TRANSWORLD PUBLISHERS
61–63 Uxbridge Road, London W5 5SA
a division of The Random House Group Ltd

RANDOM HOUSE AUSTRALIA (PTY) LTD
20 Alfred Street, Milsons Point, Sydney, New South Wales 2061, Australia

RANDOM HOUSE NEW ZEALAND LTD
18 Poland Road, Glenfield, Auckland 10, New Zealand

RANDOM HOUSE SOUTH AFRICA (PTY) LTD
Endulini, 5a Jubilee Road, Parktown 2193, South Africa

Published 2005 by Channel 4 Books, a division of Transworld Publishers

A Maverick Television Limited production for Channel 4

Text copyright © Nicky Hambleton-Jones, Alexandra Fraser and Karen Dolby 2005

The right of Nicky Hambleton-Jones, Alexandra Fraser and Karen Dolby to be
identified as the authors of this work has been asserted in accordance with
sections 77 and 78 of the Copyright, Designs and Patents Act 1988.

A catalogue record for this book is available from the British Library.

ISBN 1 905 02603 X

Designed and typeset by Smith and Gilmour, London
Photography by Mark Read
Edited by Gillian Haslam
Printed in Germany

10 9 8 7 6 5 4

Papers used by Transworld Publishers are natural, recyclable products
made from wood grown in sustainable forests. The manufacturing processes
conform to the environmental regulations of the country of origin.

To Mom, Dad and Rob, for their
unconditional love and support.

Contents

Introduction

You're probably thinking, what's the big deal? Why should I care about the number of wrinkles I have on my face? Why should I try to defy the course of time and turn back the clock? What happened to ageing gracefully? Well, I couldn't agree with you more, as long as you're truly happy with yourself and the way you look. By that I don't mean it's unacceptable to have wrinkles and we should all be booking ourselves in for face lifts. On the contrary, I believe we should all try to make the most, and the best, of what we've got. It's the small things, like brushing your teeth twice a day and wearing sunscreen, that make the biggest difference between looking good for your age and looking old for your age.

We're a skin-deep society, and one that judges people on appearance. Consciously or subconsciously, rightly or wrongly, each and every one of us has at some point passed judgement on someone else based purely on the way they look. But instead of getting depressed by this, following some or all of my advice will help you look so good that no one will give a second thought to how old you actually are. I'm talking about looking as good on the outside as you feel on the inside, presenting yourself in such a way that people's first impression is how fabulous you look.

Every day, more and more research is done on the causes of ageing and how to prevent it, but I find it far more exciting to know that eating seven prunes a day will give me all the antioxidants I need, and that 80 per cent of lines and wrinkles are caused by the environment, while only 20 per cent are genetic. That's so empowering, because it means that each of us has the ability to look amazing, whatever our age or budget. This book is filled with anti-ageing hints and tips that you can do in the comfort of your own home and on the tightest of budgets. For example, the most powerful moisturizer and anti-ageing weapon for your skin is water. We all have access to water, and it won't cost you anything, so the next time you're about to spend a fortune on a so-called 'miracle' face cream, think again. The answer isn't in a pot, it's in your tap.

Talking of miracles, I'd like to put to bed the whole concept of a quick-fix route to youthful looks. No cure is ever as good as prevention. Once the damage has been done, there's nothing out there that will restore your skin to its former glory. It may improve it, but it won't give you back what you had. So the next time you think, 'Who cares, I'll worry about it when I'm older,' you're in for a rather rude awakening.

I was one of the lucky ones. My mum is an inspirational role model and she genuinely looks younger and fantastic for her age. She instilled in me from a very young age the importance of looking after yourself. This could have totally backfired on her, and for a while it did. When you're a rebellious teenager and your mother tells you not to lie in the sun, frown or smoke*, what do you do? Everything she tells you not to! I do admire her perseverance with my ultra-strong will. Somehow she managed to penetrate my mind and I owe a lot to her. She also taught me the importance of wearing colour, and I am now the biggest advocate of doing just that.

The reason I decided to write this book is because looking 10 years younger is far more than a jab of botox, a new outfit and a trendy haircut. Although these will certainly give you a kick-start in the right direction, it's your day-to-day lifestyle that will ultimately help you fight the backlash of time. There's no point spending a fortune on expensive face creams or cosmetic surgery if you're going to smoke and lie in the sun. In fact, I'd say you're wasting your time and money. It's probably not what you want to hear, but smoking and sun damage are the two biggest culprits when it comes to premature ageing. If there's nothing else you take away from this book, all I ask is that you stop lying in the sun (and that includes sunbeds) and you stop smoking. I cannot stress enough how damaging they are for your health and your skin. The good news is that within eight hours of stubbing out your last cigarette, your nicotine levels will have halved, and within a week of wearing sun protection every day, your skin will start to improve. It's never too late to make a difference.

Now, in case you're thinking this book is all about living a purist life of deprivation in the hope of preventing a few wrinkles, let me put your

* In case you're wondering, it was only ever a couple of fags . . . and I never inhaled, promise!

mind at rest. I'm going to give you lots of ingredients to help you look, and feel, younger, but it's not a prescription. I want to help you build a foundation that will really work for you. I know from experience that some days will be easier than others. So you've had a bad week, it's all gone out the window and you just want to give up. Don't. Just because you've had a bad night's sleep doesn't mean you'll never sleep again for the rest of your life, does it? We're all human, so it's OK to fall off the wagon every now and then. Just don't make a regular habit of it.

Not everything I recommend in this book will be practical or appropriate for you. I'd rather you tried to do less but did it regularly than burned out after a month. What's important is that you look at changing the way you live for life. Small adjustments can make a big impact.

My passion in life is helping people feel better about themselves. Every day I revamp someone's wardrobe and I never cease to be amazed at the difference clothes can make to the way someone looks and feels. There are days when even I wake up feeling a little off centre with the world. The first thing I do is put on something that makes me feel slim, sexy and gorgeous. I can then leave the house with confidence, knowing I look good, even if I feel a little shaky on the inside. Fake it till you make it, I say.

Women have never had it better. We're more empowered and successful than ever before; we have a wealth of opportunities open to us and genuine life choices to make. Not so long ago we were considered on our way out at 40. Now women in their 50s and 60s are looking great, are sexually active, enjoying fantastic careers and embracing life to the full.

I hope this book will inspire you to start taking control of your life and your destiny before it's too late. The more you look after your body, the more your body will look after you.If we all made an effort to look and feel good about ourselves, just think how happy a place the world would be. If looking younger will help you feel better about yourself, then this is the book you've been waiting for. Here's to 10 years younger for life.

Nicky

the ageing process

It's definitely not a compliment to be told to 'act your age', but the last thing most people want is to actually look their age.

People are living longer than ever before. National Statistics Office figures for 2001 show life expectancy for women to be 80.6 years and 75.9 years for men. While this could be seen as one of our greatest achievements, there is no doubt that this allows plenty of time for the advancing years to begin to show.

We're all familiar with the signs of old age – wrinkles, sagging skin, an ever-expanding waistline, loss of strength, thinning hair, failing eyesight and hearing – but what most people don't realize is that although they may look and feel older, their body is actually continuously renewing itself. Blood is replaced every three months, and parts of the skeleton every few years. At any one time, most of your body will be no more than 10 years old. Sadly, it just doesn't look or feel that way. It may be that in constantly copying itself, the body develops weaknesses and faults, or simply that over the years it's attacked and damaged by free radicals in the air we breathe, the environment in which we live and the food we eat.

So what happens to your face and body as it matures? In short, what is ageing? The hand your genes have dealt you is obviously very important when it comes to the way you look, but so is your lifestyle. Smoking and drinking, your diet, the amount of exercise you take, stress and exposure to the sun all help to determine just how well you age.

IT'S A FACT
Only 10–20 per cent of lines are unavoidable; the rest are down to you and environmental factors.

DID YOU KNOW?
The single most important thing you can do for your skin is to protect it from the sun. 80–90 per cent of all signs of ageing may be due to exposure to sunlight.

HOW WILL THE DECADES
AFFECT YOU?

Thrilled to be 30, fab at 40, fit at 50, feel like you've never looked better. The pressure is on to look fantastic whatever your age. Even 30 years ago, looking older was accepted as inevitable, but this is no longer the case. We're bombarded with images of glamorous celebrities defying the signs of ageing or the fact that they've recently given birth, looking as slim, gorgeous and wrinkle-free as the day they first hit our screens decades earlier.

Don't despair. Just by understanding your body and how it changes over time, you too can make a difference and look and feel younger.

In your 20s

No one in their early 20s really wants to look ten years younger, but many people would like to preserve their youthful appearance. This is an important decade in terms of setting the foundations for looking younger later in life. You're never too young to moisturize and protect your skin, eat healthily, exercise and kick those bad habits.

FACT FILE

- Skin begins the ageing process between the ages of 17 and 25

- The beauty industry judges skin to be 'mature' from the late 20s onwards

- Though you may not notice, skin damage starts early in childhood

- From your 20s onwards your metabolism and muscle mass decline while body fat increases

- Any excess fat is generally evenly distributed around your body at this stage

- Between the ages of 20 and 25 cell renewal drops by up to 28 per cent and your cells divide more slowly

- Bones stop growing in your mid-20s

- At 20, most people's hair is the thickest it will ever be

- Male pattern baldness and loss of hair pigment follow fast

- By the end of the decade women's skin becomes less oily and the first wrinkles may make an appearance

Take action

- Your 20s can be a fabulous time for your skin. Hormones have usually settled, while your skin still has that youthful glow that older generations envy. But if you want to keep your face and body looking great, you need to set up some good habits now.

- Most importantly, moisturize and protect your skin from the sun. Make sure you wear a cream with at least SPF 15 every day, and increase this to a specific sun-protection cream with a higher factor on sunny days or when you're on holiday. And don't forget your neck and the backs of your hands, which are just as exposed as your face.

- As cell renewal slows, your skin can look dull, and it helps to use a gentle exfoliant. It's also not unusual for acne to continue into your 20s. If it's a problem, it's worth talking to an expert, as you may need specialist treatment.

- Nothing ages you faster than smoking. By the time they are 30, smokers can look 10 years older. Smoke breaks down collagen and elastin, and deprives the skin of oxygen and moisture, dulling the complexion and causing wrinkles, including the puckered lines around the mouth that are characteristic of heavy smokers.

- If you really can't kick the habit, use a good antioxidant cream with vitamins A, C and E to help counteract some of the effects.

- What you eat now affects your health and how well you age. When you're busy, it's very easy to eat on the run, grabbing quick convenience food. But too much sugar, salt and processed food can cause a range of problems later in life, including diabetes, heart disease, osteoporosis and even cancer. Yo-yo dieting is also to be avoided as skin becomes overstretched, making it look saggy and wrinkled. Try to eat a balanced diet, including more fresh fruit and vegetables. As your bones don't stop growing until your mid-20s a good supply of calcium and omega-3 fatty acids is also vital (see pages 171 and 175).

- Exercise and good posture will make you look and feel better, both now and later in life. If you can't face the gym, try walking part of the way to work and take the stairs instead of the lift.

DID YOU KNOW?

The dermis gradually thins after the age of 25, when we begin to lose collagen at a rate of roughly 1.5 per cent a year.

In your 30s

Although the first real signs of ageing begin to make an appearance during this decade, there's no reason why you shouldn't look and feel fantastic. It's a cliché, but as well as being older, you're also wiser. You know what suits you and what works best for you – with the additional help of this book! – but an increasingly busy lifestyle can bring its own stresses and strains. By adjusting your diet you can maintain your ideal shape, boost your energy levels and keep stress in check. Weight-bearing exercise helps maintain your metabolic rate, as well as tackling problems that begin at this stage, such as cellulite, fluid retention, hormonal swings and blood-sugar imbalances.

'Ageing really begins at 30.'

DR MARY ELLEN BRADAMAS, NEW YORK DERMATOLOGIST

FACT FILE

---> Any extra weight tends to head for the hips on most women

---> You lose 3.2 kg of lean body mass each decade and your body burns energy 2–4 per cent more slowly

---> 'Only 10 per cent of lines are unavoidable. The rest are environmental,' says Tracey Nathan, MD of NV Perricone Cosmeceuticals, one of America's leading anti-ageing cream manufacturers

---> Cell renewal slows, so you lose that youthful radiance. Oil glands also become less active, making skin drier

---> Sun spots and uneven pigmentation can appear in your late 30s

---> Environmental damage, including smoking, sunlight and pollution, begins to take its toll, causing collagen fibres to loosen

---> Collagen and elastin start to break down and more fine lines develop

---> From your mid-30s you have the classic choice – preserve your face or your bottom. If you lose too much weight, your face will lose the layer of fat just beneath the surface that helps to fill out wrinkles, making them appear less obvious

---> The delicate skin around the eyes begins to thin

---> Broken veins may begin to show as red dots

---> One in three women over the age of 30 in the UK now uses anti-ageing products

Take action

⋯⋗ It's now even more important to maintain a balanced diet rich in antioxidants and vitamins A, B, C and E to help fight the effects of free radicals.

⋯⋗ Alongside sun protection, it's a good idea to use a face cream that contains antioxidants. As your skin will probably be drier now, you will need a richer moisturizer, and it's important to use a specific eye cream.

⋯⋗ Exfoliation or a gentle face peel (see page 53) can help combat skin dullness.

⋯⋗ A sensible exercise regime, preferably including some weight-bearing exercise to maintain muscle strength, will help fight flab and boost your energy levels.

⋯⋗ Eating less salt and more potassium-rich foods, such as bananas, grains, potatoes and dried fruit, will help combat cellulite and fluid retention.

⋯⋗ Avoid drinking too much alcohol, especially if you want to halt the development of red spider veins. Plenty of water will keep you hydrated and healthy-looking.

⋯⋗ Hormone levels can vary, and you may notice a swing in blood-sugar levels. Avoid sugary, processed foods and replace them with more complex carbohydrates. Vitamin-rich foods will also help.

⋯⋗ Bodybrushing before a shower boosts circulation and tackles cellulite.

⋯⋗ You can no longer hope to get away with very little sleep, as this is the time when your body repairs itself.

In your 40s

Ageing really starts in earnest during this decade, with physical changes accelerating, especially for women approaching the menopause. What you do now plays a vital role in how young you. Sun protection is even more important, and as cell renewal slows and the skin becomes more fragile, using a moisturizer with antioxidants will help protect against damage from free radicals. Your metabolic rate and digestive system slow, but eating the right foods and taking regular exercise will help combat the effects.

'A bit of lusting after someone does wonders for the skin.'

ELIZABETH HURLEY, MODEL AND ACTRESS

···➔ If you eat as much or in the same way as you did in your 20s, you can't expect to remain the same size and shape

···➔ The physical differences between men and women increase with age (see page 28)

···➔ Your skin loses its resilience as more collagen and elastin are lost. So if you lose weight too quickly, excess skin will become baggy

···➔ Women burn calories more slowly than men and their bodies have a naturally higher fat content

···➔ The loss of subcutaneous fat, which cushions the skin and forms its foundation, leaves skin more fragile

···➔ In your late 40s oestrogen levels in women fall, adding to the loss of moisture, collagen and elastin

···➔ Oil production falls dramatically and most women's skin is drier

···➔ Lines and wrinkles become more definite, particularly on the forehead and around the eyes

···➔ Dead skin cells can build up on the surface layer of the skin, roughening its texture

···➔ Skin thins as you get older (apart from the dead surface layer), making wrinkles more visible and cellulite more obvious

···➔ Avoid jogging if you want to preserve a youthful face and profile (see Chapter 5 – The Body)

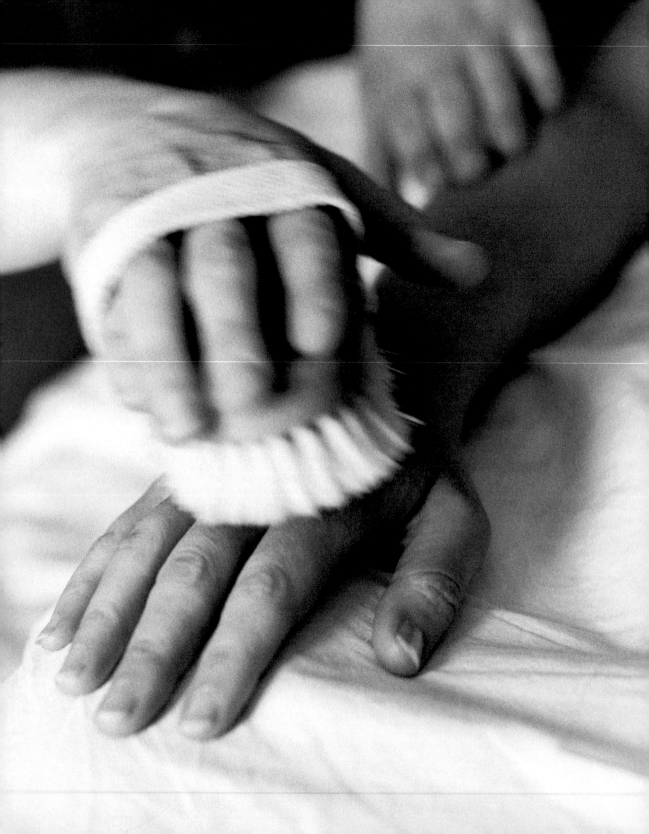

Take action

--→ There are growing numbers of anti-ageing products available that are specifically designed to limit damage and help you hold back the years (see Chapter 4 – Beauty).

--→ Your skin will become gradually drier and rougher from now on, so exfoliation is important. It's also critical to carry on protecting your skin against sun damage if you want to avoid sun spots, uneven pigmentation and even more wrinkles.

--→ A good defence against damage from free radicals is vital. Use a moisturizer rich in antioxidants.

--→ Vitamin A and retinoids will help boost collagen and elastin levels in your skin, making it look younger.

--→ Exercise is even more important to maintain a healthy skeleton and muscle tone, and to combat a slower metabolism. A combination of weight-bearing or resistance exercise and a cardiovascular workout is best.

--→ It's not always easy to avoid stress, especially as most people in their 40s have hectic lifestyles, balancing the needs of family, home and work. But there's no doubt that your body will now cope less well with stress and lack of sleep, so be gentle with yourself and make sure you have enough time to rest and recover from everyday life.

--→ Now is the time to take a good, long look at your diet. What you ate even a decade ago may no longer suit your body's needs. Hormone and oestrogen-balancing foods are key if you want to feel healthy and avoid the worst effects of ageing.

Your 50s and beyond

With greater self-knowledge, better skincare, regular exercise and a balanced diet, there's no reason why men and women shouldn't remain healthy and look stunning well past middle age. Celebrities like Catherine Deneuve, Tina Turner and Paul Newman are just a few famous examples of how to age well. There has never been more choice available, and today's typical 50-year-old is far from winding down into retirement or old age. With more freedom and, with any luck, less of the lifestyle stresses you faced in your 40s, this is a time to enjoy yourself.

Take action

⋯⋗ As well as being more fragile, your skin will also be much more sensitive to pollutants and allergens, but with a little extra care there's no reason why it shouldn't remain healthy and glowing. Choose rich anti-ageing creams to moisturize and restore balance.

⋯⋗ Gentle products to slough away dead skin cells and stimulate collagen help maintain a youthful appearance.

⋯⋗ Staying out of the sun is still crucial if you want an even skin tone and don't want sun spots to worsen.

⋯⋗ Exercise is important, but avoid straining muscles and joints: practise yoga or take a swim.

FACT FILE

---> Fewer calories are burned and more are stored as fat. The average 70-year-old needs 500 fewer calories a day than a 25-year-old

---> After the menopause, the drop in oestrogen levels triggers a change in a woman's shape and weight. More weight accumulates on your hips, for example, and breasts get bigger, usually reaching a peak between the ages of 55 and 64, and shrinking again after the age of 65

---> Extra fat tends to head for the waist and stay put

---> An average 65-year-old woman is about 43 per cent fat, while at 25 she was 25 per cent fat. The average 65-year-old man is 38 per cent fat, while at 25 he was 18 per cent fat

---> Oestrogen levels fall after the menopause, which means skin becomes thinner and more fragile, and skin tone tends to become more uneven

---> Melamolytes, or pigment cells, clump together, causing the number of sun spots on your skin to increase. The skin also tends to lose pigment as you get older, and the number of individual melamolytes drops

---> The lines you develop now may deepen into folds, and the skin may begin to sag and droop due to a loss of fat tissue under the skin

---> Women may notice an increase in facial hair, again as a result of the drop in oestrogen and rise in testosterone levels

---> As skin ages, it becomes more fragile and less sensitive, making it prone to damage and bruising

The differences between men and women

It's sad but true. The old adage that men age better than women does have some basis in medical fact.

Because men produce more of the sex hormone androgen, the middle and lower layers of their skin are thicker, making them less prone to wrinkles and other signs of ageing. They also have added protection from the extra oil in their skin generated by testosterone. When testosterone levels begin to fall, which can happen from 35 onwards, men start to show more signs of ageing.

As previously discussed, women also tend naturally to have more fat, and the difference just keeps widening with age.

However, there is good news for women as far as hair is concerned. Although women's hair thins to some degree after the menopause, when they lose the female hormone oestrogen and produce more testosterone, early baldness is still very much a male phenomenon, as is the abundant extra growth of hair in the nostrils and ears, to say nothing of those bushy eyebrows.

Anti-ageing

There's no doubt that we've come a long way in the last 20 years. At least in theory, we know what goes towards giving us a healthy lifestyle, and we know some of the things we should avoid. The interest in anti-ageing has never been greater. Open a woman's magazine and you'll doubtless find a number of adverts for products claiming to lift, firm and fill fine lines or reduce the appearance of wrinkles, and that's before you start

reading the articles on defying the ageing process or the secret of youth. But then we are an ageing population. If current trends continue, the proportion of people over 60 will rise to 34 per cent in the UK by 2050 (it now stands at 21 per cent), and while there's never been more choice of product or treatment available, there's also never been so much pressure on us to look younger for longer.

My ten steps to a more youthful you

1. Don't smoke Nothing ages you faster.

2. Adjust your diet Eat at least five portions of fruit and vegetables, and boost your intake of omega-3 essential fatty acids and antioxidants (see page 181). Avoid processed, sugary foods and drink plenty of water.

3. Exercise A toned supple body will not only help to make you look younger, but regular exercise will make you feel and act younger too.

4. Moderate your alcohol intake However, remember that a glass of red wine is good for your heart. It also contains all-important antioxidants to help your body fight ageing free radicals, and even contains a compound called resveratrol to stimulate lean cells and help shed fat. Now there's something to make you smile!

5. Cleanse, moisturize and protect your skin every day Change the products you use – look at what's new and what's suitable for you at the age you are now.

6. Get a good night's sleep

7. Reduce stress levels Take time out to relax. Try yoga, massage, meditation, soak in a scented bath, or whatever it takes to help you unwind.

8. Smile and be confident There's no surer way to shed the years.

9. Adapt your style Don't get stuck in a rut. Regularly overhaul your wardrobe, cosmetics, hairstyle and colour.

10. Increase your fresh air and oxygen intake Take a country walk or cycle ride – you'll be exercising at the same time.

DID YOU KNOW?
Laughter is good for your skin. It tones the muscles and boosts circulation, giving you a natural, healthy glow.

the face

CHAPTER TWO

From a distance I might look at a person's body shape, the way they walk, their clothes or their hair to gauge their age, but when I meet someone, the first thing I notice is their face, and I don't think I'm unusual in this. You can disguise your body with a little know-how, and a trip to a good stylist will sort out your hair, but your face is always on show and it's the hardest place to cheat the years. Eyes, teeth, nose, neck and, perhaps most crucially, skin all give clues to a person's age. But while you know your age, it is possible to leave others wondering. You may not be able to stop the advancing years, but you can determine how quickly they begin to show.

'Nature gives you the face you have at 20; it's up to you to merit the face you have at 50.'

COCO CHANEL, COUTURIER AND DESIGNER

SKIN

The skin is one of the most complex organs in the body. An average adult has 2 square metres of skin, which weighs 3.2kg and is composed of around 300 million skin cells. There is an outer layer, or epidermis, a middle layer of fibrous tissue called the dermis, and beneath this a layer of subcutaneous fat.

Skin types

There are two main types of human skin – hairy and non-hairy or glabrous skin. The palms of the hands and soles of the feet are covered by glabrous skin, with its characteristic thick epidermis and fingerprints.

Hairy skin varies according to where it is. For instance, the scalp is very different from the face. It also contains various other structures within it. Sebaceous oil glands are attached to hair follicles, and sweat glands are found in the dermis, with ducts passing through the epidermis to the skin's surface. There are also blood vessels, nerves and sense organs.

Top of the list when it comes to cosmetic skin concerns are wrinkles. We are bombarded with airbrushed images of perfection, so is it any wonder that we've come to view our natural image critically? But just how well we age is not beyond our control. It's not just a question of genes but how we choose to live our lives. Our skin begins the ageing process between the ages of 17 and 25, but up to 80 per cent of all signs of ageing – including wrinkles, sun spots or uneven pigmentation and spider veins – are down to environment, and that means exposure to sunlight, smoking and our general lifestyle.

DID YOU KNOW?
When clinicians refer to living skin they're talking about the dermis, the middle layer of the skin.

DID YOU KNOW?
A 12mm square of skin contains on average:
10 hairs, 15 sebaceous glands, 100 sweat glands and 1 metre of tiny blood capillaries.

SKIN FACTS

→ Collagen makes up 70 per cent of the skin

→ Collagen is the main structural protein in the skin, and its fibres act as scaffolding to give skin strength and maintain elasticity

→ Vitamin C is essential for the production of collagen

→ Elastin, which is the skin's other main fibrous protein, gives skin its bounce

→ Collagen production is badly affected by sun damage, smoking and eating too much sugar, causing wrinkling and sagging

→ Collagen and elastin fibres become less flexible over time because of damage by free radicals

→ Antioxidant vitamins A, C and E and minerals such as selenium limit damage caused by free radicals

→ A normal skin should be composed of roughly 70 per cent living cells and 30 per cent dead cells

→ At the age of 40, only 30 per cent of skin cells are still active

→ The epidermis never stops growing from the bottom layer up

→ Dead skin cells are usually shed invisibly from the surface (the dead cell layer is called the *stratum corneum*)

→ On average it takes between 52 and 75 days for a complete cycle from the development of new skin cells until they are shed

→ Essential fatty acids (such as those in seeds, nuts and oily fish) are vital for healthy skin to maintain the membranes of skin cells

Stop the clock

If you do nothing else, these three steps will halt the development of lines and give you a healthier, younger-looking complexion:

⋯▸ Avoid overexposure to the sun and *always* use a sunscreen.
⋯▸ Don't smoke.
⋯▸ It's never too late or too soon to implement a good skincare routine. Start today and stick to it.

Sunlight and skin

When you look in the mirror, 80 per cent of the wrinkles you see are probably caused by sun damage. Professor Chris Griffiths of the Dermatology Research Group at the University of Manchester believes UVA rays are the main culprits responsible for photo-ageing, although UVB plays some part. This is because UVA penetrates deeper into the skin and breaks down the collagen-forming cells or fibroblasts. The sun also dehydrates the skin and causes uneven pigmentation, or sun spots, to develop – a real giveaway when it comes to age.

In many ways I was lucky. Growing up in South Africa meant we were always aware of the dangers of sunburn. My mother made sure I wore sunblock and avoided the sun entirely during the hottest part of the day.

Sun damage can be seen immediately as sunburn, but the more serious effects are often cumulative and may only be noticed years later. These long-term effects include freckles, sun spots, wrinkles, coarse skin texture and spider veins. There are also serious health implications. Reports from Cancer Research UK show that the UK now has more skin-cancer deaths than Australia. This is because many people don't know what danger signs to look out for. If you spot any changes in moles or skin pigmentation, *always* check with your GP. People with fair skins are obviously the most affected, but no one is immune.

DID YOU KNOW?

50 per cent of your total UV radiation is acquired by the age of 18, and 75 per cent by the age of 30.

Sun facts

⟩ The sun's rays are at their most intense between 10 a.m. and 3 p.m. At other times the atmosphere filters out more of their damaging energy.

⟩ At high altitudes the atmosphere is thinner and more harmful rays reach us.

⟩ For every 30 metres increase in altitude the sun's rays are roughly 5 per cent more powerful.

⟩ Sunscreens are categorized by a Sun Protection Factor or SPF. The higher the SPF, the greater the protection.

⟩ As a guide, if your skin usually burns after 15 minutes in the sun, an SPF of 20 will extend that 15 minutes by 20.

DID YOU KNOW?
You should protect your neck using a high SPF if you want to avoid horizontal lines – the skin on your neck is thinner than your face, so it shows sun damage more quickly. ⟩⟩ The sun can age your skin by up to 20 years. ⟩⟩ Much of the sun damage done to our skins happens by chance whenever we're outside going about our daily lives. ⟩⟩ The only safe tan is a fake tan.

Common myths about sunscreens

So much has been written and broadcast about the importance of using sun protection that it's a wonder we're not all experts. I've lost count of the number of times clients have asked me the same questions, and I'd like to lay these myths to rest once and for all.

MYTH: I'm a real sun lover. I used to lie in the sun for hours in my 20s, so the damage is already done. Surely there's no point in using a high SPF now?
REALITY: If anything it's even more important. You don't want to do any more damage to your skin, and think of the health risks.

MYTH: The sun isn't shining, so do I need to wear sunscreen?
REALITY: Don't be fooled by cloudy summer days or wintry skies. UV rays can still penetrate and damage skin. I always use at least factor 15 sun protection either in my moisturizer or foundation, and if I know I'm going to be outside for some time, or when I'm on holiday, I choose a much higher factor sunblock, at least an SPF 30.

MYTH: By sticking to the shade I'll avoid the risk of burning.
REALITY: The sun's rays are reflected by water, sand and snow, so sitting in the shade is no guarantee of protection.

MYTH: My sunscreen is waterproof, so I don't need to reapply it after swimming.
REALITY: All sun products need reapplying every two hours. Protection disappears from the skin through normal movement and certainly after swimming.

MYTH: Wearing sunscreen gives me spots.
REALITY: Sometimes sunscreen mixed with heat and sweat can block pores, so if you suffer a breakout, switch to a non-greasy lotion or cream and make sure you cleanse thoroughly and shower off at night.

MYTH: The chemicals in sunscreen irritate my skin.
REALITY: Sensitive skin can react to chemicals; if yours does, choose one of the growing number of mineral sunscreens, such as titanium dioxide or zinc oxide. These remain on the skin's surface, creating a physical barrier that isn't absorbed, thus reducing the danger of irritation.

MYTH: If I use a high protection factor, I won't get a tan.
REALITY: You will just build up your tan more slowly and without the burn. The good news is that your tan will last longer and you won't experience any unsightly peeling or nasty ageing effects.

Choosing sunscreen

---> Choose a product that offers broad-spectrum UVA and UVB protection.

---> Look for one that also contains antioxidants to neutralize damaging free radicals generated through exposure to the sun.

---> More mature skin benefits from the addition of essential fatty acids to rehydrate skin.

---> If you prefer to avoid chemicals, there are increasing numbers of products that use natural mineral sunscreens, such as titanium dioxide and zinc oxide, which act as a physical barrier. These are particularly suitable for sensitive skin.

---> Mineral filter sunscreens work by reflecting and scattering light and are not absorbed by the skin. Chemical filters sink into the skin and absorb the sun's rays, which can lead to photochemical skin reactions.

---> Look for melatonin-boosting plant ingredients and moisturizing, soothing oils, such as jojoba.

---> Antioxidant vitamins, such as E and C, will help to strengthen and repair skin, stimulating cell renewal. Vitamin A also helps to protect from damage.

Applying sunscreen

---> Don't forget ears, nose, eyelids, lips and the base of your neck– they're all very exposed and prone to burning.

---> If you're using a chemical sunscreen, apply it 20 minutes before venturing out into the sun, so that your skin has time to absorb it.

---> Mineral screens work immediately on application because they form a barrier on the skin's surface.

---> Reapply sunscreen every two hours when the sun is hot.

---> When you're out in the sun it's even more important to drink plenty of water to hydrate your skin, and boosting the vitamins and essential fatty acids you eat will help protect your skin from the inside too.

STOP PRESS!
It's not all bad news. Everyone feels happier when the sun is shining, and provided we protect ourselves from overexposure, sunlight is good for you. It also helps form vitamin D in the skin, which is essential for healthy, strong bones.

Smoking and skin

Whatever your age, whatever your lifestyle, there is one thing you can do to keep your skin looking younger and that is don't smoke. Sorry, I know it isn't easy to give up, but there really is nothing more ageing – and I won't even start on the damage you're doing to your health. I can tell at a glance whether a new client is a smoker or not – they're generally more lined and there's a dull, grey pallor to even the most outdoorsy of faces. But you don't have to take *my* word for it, the facts speak for themselves.

THE FACTS

⋯➔ According to Dr Miriam Stoppard, the face of a 20-a-day smoker ages 14 years for every 10 years of smoking

⋯➔ Smokers in their 40s often have as many wrinkles as non-smokers in their 60s

⋯➔ Smokers look older than non-smokers because tobacco smoke triggers an enzyme that attacks the skin's elasticity, breaking down collagen

⋯➔ Smokers who sunbathe wrinkle even faster, as UV rays accelerate the production of this anti-collagen protein

⋯➔ Research shows smoking can reduce the production of collagen by up to 40 per cent

⋯➔ Once collagen has been destroyed, it's gone for ever (although a medium face peel stimulates your fibroblasts to produce more collagen, see page 60). As you get older, the number of fibroblasts in your skin diminishes and the remaining ones become less active. Smoking speeds up this process

→ Tobacco smoke has a drying effect on the skin's surface and causes stress lines, particularly around the mouth and eyes

→ Smoke is an irritant so smokers tend to squint and wrinkle their eyes, giving them lines that eventually become permanent

→ As well as puckering around the mouth from drawing on a cigarette, smokers also often develop hollow cheeks

→ Smoke restricts blood vessels and so reduces blood flow to the skin, robbing it of oxygen and nutrients

→ Smokers lose 35mg more vitamin C a day than non-smokers. Vitamin C is a powerful antioxidant, and is vitally important in boosting our body's immunity and protecting against ageing free radicals

→ Research also suggests that smoke reduces the body's store of vitamin A, which helps protect against skin-damaging agents produced by tobacco smoke

→ Smoking has a particularly noticeable effect on women's skin as it's usually thinner, so wrinkles show sooner and are more obvious

→ The good news is that if you stop now, you'll also stop the damage to your collagen levels, you'll immediately boost your flagging circulation and will see obvious improvements in your skin after just two weeks

→ Nicotine and carbon monoxide levels in your body are halved just eight hours after giving up

ESTABLISHING A GOOD SKINCARE ROUTINE

Don't worry, I'm not suggesting you spend hours on your face. I'm a firm believer in not doing any more than you have to, but you really will see the benefits of a sensible routine that suits you and that you're happy to stick to. The right skincare will set you up for the day and help your skin to recover at night, which are both vital if you want your skin to remain clear and youthful.

I'm not a particular believer in fancy, expensive products. There's only so much you can do with creams, but I do think it's worth taking time to find products that suit you and that you enjoy using. The right cream will glide into your skin, leaving it softer and feeling more comfortable. Plus if you enjoy the sensation of the cream being smoothed on and its smell, you're going to feel happier, which in turn will make you feel and look younger.

There are now several shops where you can get independent advice on several different product ranges. Alternatively, don't be afraid to ask at a number of beauty counters and *always* ask for samples before buying a whole pot or bottle. It's worth checking what new products are on the market and whether your skin would benefit from a change. Your skin doesn't remain the same and it will need different treatments at different times.

I advise making seasonal adjustments to your skincare. I always change the products I use according to the season. For instance, in the summer I need a lighter moisturizer than in the winter, but a higher sun protection factor is a must. As a general rule, most people's skin is drier in winter and needs a more intense moisturizer because of harsher weather and greater extremes of temperature, with cold winds outside and hot, dry central heating indoors.

My routine

⋯⋗ Always cleanse your face and neck thoroughly. In the morning, cleansing helps freshen and prepare your skin.

⋯⋗ Follow with a moisturizer. This helps to seal in moisture and hydration, and protects your skin from the environment. I always use one with SPF 15 in winter and SPF 30 in summer.

⋯⋗ Even oily skin needs moisturizing to lock in water and keep it hydrated, otherwise normal enzyme activity will slow down, leaving skin prone to irritation.

⋯⋗ Cleansing and moisturizing your skin well will give you a good base for any other cosmetics you use, making them look better and last longer.

⋯⋗ At night it's even more important to cleanse skin to remove all the dirt it's accumulated through the day. I couldn't even think about going to bed without removing my make-up first. It's one of the first things my mother taught me to do when I began taking an interest in make-up. It only takes a minute, and as night time is when skin repairs and rejuvenates itself, it's vital your skin should be able to breathe. I really think this is the key if you want to keep signs of ageing at bay.

⋯⋗ Moisturize again. Your skin loses more water at night and it's also more receptive to nourishment. I usually use the same moisturizer as during the day, but some people prefer to use a specific night cream. This may be a good idea if your skin is dry or sensitive, and as you get older you may want to use a more intense anti-ageing product with extra antioxidants. It's important not to use too rich a cream, though, as you don't want to block your pores.

⋯⋗ Once a week I exfoliate my skin to remove dead cells. This is essential if you want to keep your complexion bright, glowing and youthful. Facial peels also help to stimulate collagen.

⋯⋗ I always follow exfoliation with a deep moisturizing mask.

DID YOU KNOW?
You can gently exfoliate your skin after cleansing using a soft washcloth or flannel. Massage your face gently using circular movements. » Using tepid water helps avoid broken capillaries.

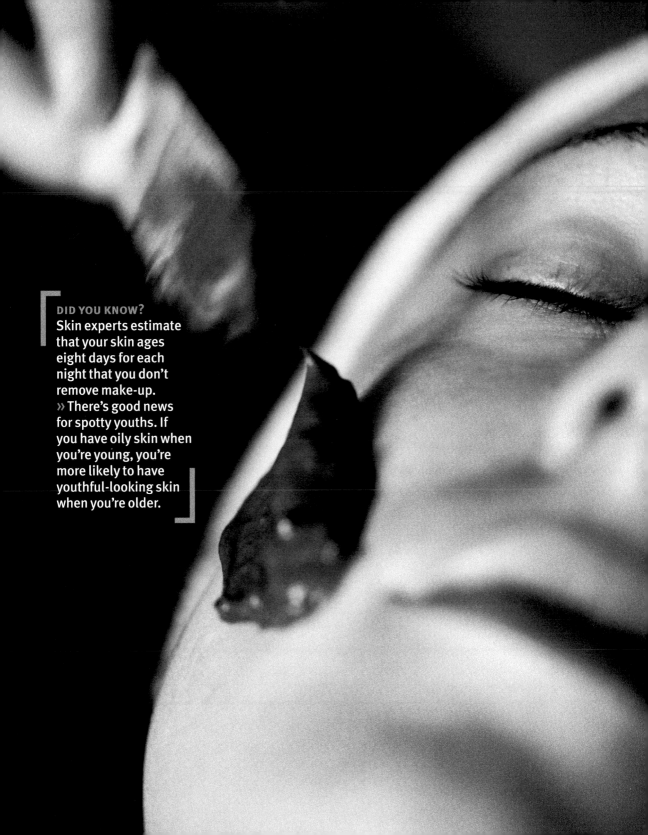

Top tips for holding back the years

···❯ Drink plenty of water – it's your skin's most important beauty treatment. About 2 litres a day will keep skin hydrated and help plump out fine lines. You'll notice a difference within hours.

···❯ Skin experts recommend sleeping on your back to encourage blood flow and reduce puffiness. You're also more likely to develop deeper wrinkles on the side of your face on which you sleep.

···❯ Easier said than done, but try to avoid stress. It triggers the release of cortisol in your body, which weakens your immune system and the skin's ability to act as a barrier, leaving it prone to inflammation and irritation.

···❯ Skin problems are often a sign of an unhealthy gut. A balanced, nutritious diet is vital if you want healthy skin. Vitamins A, C and E and essential fatty acids are particularly important in the fight against premature skin ageing (see Chapter 7 – Nutrition).

···❯ Treat yourself to regular facials. They help to relax muscles and tone the complexion. They are also a good way of keeping up to date with new products and understanding what your skin is like now.

'I'm basically a Vaseline and cotton bud girl…but I always use anti-ageing products – I see it as preventative.'

SCARLETT JOHANSSON, ACTRESS

Anti-ageing skin creams

As our obsession with looking younger longer grows, scientists and dermatologists continue to research effective anti-ageing treatments. They have discovered a number of vitamins and natural ingredients to help slow down the ageing process and that may even reverse some of the signs of ageing skin. No cream can work an overnight miracle, but regular use should ensure a gradual improvement over a number of weeks.

Vitamin A can help to puff up the skin and fill out fine lines.

Vitamin C is a powerful antioxidant. It heals and boosts collagen production and circulation. It generally brightens the skin.

Vitamin E is another powerful antioxidant and moisturizer.

Retinoids are chemicals that encourage the production of new skin cells, giving skin a smoother appearance.

Alpha hydroxy acids (or AHAs) encourage the skin to shed dead surface cells, improving texture and reducing large pores. They are particularly useful for oily or acne-prone skin.

Copper peptides improve elasticity, reduce fine lines and help firm the skin. Copper is part of an enzyme involved in the production of melanin.

Green tea extract is an antioxidant and anti-inflammatory. It's good to drink and is effective topically to reduce puffiness, wrinkles and large pores.

Anti-ageing skincare treatments

However hard we try, we can't stop all the signs of skin ageing, and nor should we want to. It's a mistake to think that the only beautiful face is a young, unlined one. As the French actress Catherine Deneuve – still lovely and well into her 50s – commented, 'I have a reasonable attitude towards my appearance. I think it's right to fight some things, but I don't want to swim against the tide, the flow of time. I want to control it a little, of course, but I don't want to be in denial.' In taking control, however, sometimes we need some extra help.

I find it helps to divide skincare into long-term strategies, medium-term treatments and short-term fixes.

Long-term strategies are all about prevention and care – all the elements I've covered so far, including a healthy diet, using a sunscreen, not smoking, drinking lots of water and establishing a good daily skincare routine of thorough cleansing and moisturizing.

Medium-term treatments won't give you instant results but you will see noticeable improvements in anything up to six months. I include in this category non-invasive cosmetic treatments such as peels, intense pulsed light therapy, and the more holistic approaches to anti-ageing skincare, such as non-surgical face lifts, facial massage, exercise and acupuncture.

Short-term fixes are more extreme cosmetic surgery procedures that, after the initial recovery period, will give you instant results. I include laser skin resurfacing and face lifts (whether brow, eye, lower or full face). I also include botox injections, fillers and chemical peels which, although they're non-invasive, should still be taken seriously and require a qualified doctor.

DID YOU KNOW?
According to market research company Mintel, 36 per cent of women in the UK now use anti-ageing creams. >> In 2002, 72,000 people in the UK turned to cosmetic surgery as a solution.

Brow softener

Soothes and calms tension in the head, forehead and eyes. Helps to soften vertical lines between the eyebrows.

⋯⋗ Place your three middle fingers between your eyebrows.

⋯⋗ Close your eyes and visualize skin-rejuvenating magnetic pulses coming out of your fingertips and into your skin. Really feel the tension being released from this area.

⋯⋗ Hold this position for one minute and repeat as often as you want.

Cheek lift

Tones, lifts and drains the cheek area.

STEP 1

⋯⋗ Pinch the cheekbone, placing your thumb firmly underneath the bone and two fingers on top. Starting at the corner of your nose, hold firmly for a count of 10 to energize the muscle.

⋯⋗ Using this method, steadily work your way to the side of the face – do this only once.

STEP 2

⋯⋗ Pinch along your cheekbone as above, but hold for only a second.

⋯⋗ Repeat three times.

Jaw firmer

Firms, tones and drains.

⋯⋗ Repeat the cheek routine, as below left, to the jaw bone.

⋯⋗ Work with both hands from the centre of the jaw outwards to under the ear.

TIP: for both the cheek and the jaw, press the thumb firmly in an upward direction.

These exercises should be repeated regularly every day and are most effective at night before bed. This is the time when cells naturally regenerate, and the massage is also relaxing so it aids restful sleep. For an extra treat, try using almond oil with a drop of lavender, frankincense or rose otto essential oils. But remember that essential oils are very potent and should always be used with care and be well diluted.

DID YOU KNOW?
It takes 62 muscles to frown and just 26 to smile.

Short-term fixes

Only a few years ago cosmetic surgery was still relatively unusual in the UK, but with the introduction of less radical, non-invasive procedures, it's becoming increasingly commonplace. Most people aren't interested in radical changes; they just want to hold back the more obvious signs of ageing and preserve a soft, youthful face.

The growth in demand for surgery brings some problems. It's impossible to walk along any high street without seeing 'clinics' offering a variety of treatments, but are they the best places to go? And how do you know if the cosmetic doctor you see is really qualified?

DID YOU KNOW?

Botox is now so popular there are botox parties, where a doctor treats a whole group of friends, just like the Tupperware parties of the 70s or the Ann Summers' parties of the 90s. » By the end of 2004 the market for cosmetic procedures will have reached almost £256 million. » BUPA Hospitals saw the number of face lifts performed increase by 38 per cent between 2002 and 2003.

'I believe in loyalty. When a woman reaches an age she likes, she should stick with it.'

EVA GABOR, ACTRESS

Choosing a qualified cosmetic surgeon

It's vital to find a qualified consultant who can properly assess your needs and explain the procedure and any side effects before you commit to surgery. Even non-invasive treatments, such as botox and laser surgery, need experienced, qualified cosmetic doctors to perform them if you are to achieve the results you want safely.

All surgeons in the UK should be registered with the General Medical Council. Professor David Sharpe, former president of the British Association of Aesthetic Plastic Surgeons (BAAPS), says, 'The only two UK associations whose members are all GMC-registered are BAAPS and the British Association of Plastic Surgeons.' Both of these organizations will give you advice on surgeons and procedures. You can also contact the General Medical Council for information about a particular surgeon's qualifications (addresses and contact numbers can be found in the directory on page 280).

Your checklist for choosing a cosmetic surgeon

⋯▹ Make sure the surgeon you choose is listed on the General Medical Council register.
⋯▹ Check what qualifications your surgeon has.
⋯▹ Ask how many operations or procedures they carry out each year.
⋯▹ Ask how experienced they are at performing your procedure.
⋯▹ Ask to see photographs showing the results they have achieved.
⋯▹ Make sure you're given full details of the treatment, including the results you can expect, any possible side effects or complications, how long the procedure will take, the recovery period and what you will need to do to assist recovery.
⋯▹ Be sure this is the right procedure for you at the age you are and with the lifestyle you lead.
⋯▹ Check how much scarring there will be.
⋯▹ Find out how long the improvement will last.
⋯▹ Take time to think about what you're doing before you commit to anything.
⋯▹ Ask what happens if things go wrong, and assess the risks.
⋯▹ Trust your gut instincts. If you have any doubts or concerns, get another opinion.

DID YOU KNOW?
However careful you are in choosing a qualified surgeon, remember no operation is risk free. » More than £7 million compensation has been paid out over the last 13 years for cosmetic surgery that has gone wrong.

Non-invasive anti-ageing treatments

Botox

Botox injections contain poisonous botulinum toxin, which is injected into the corrugator facial muscles to paralyse them, the idea being that because the muscles can't move, they can't form or deepen wrinkles. It's usually used to reduce or relax frown lines, forehead lines and crow's feet around the eyes. The toxin cannot cause any permanent damage or travel around the body because it attaches itself to the muscle where it was injected. It is then destroyed by the body after 3–6 months.

Initially there can be some bruising at the injection site or tiny red pinpricks. The injection gradually takes effect over the following five to ten days, giving the face a smoother, rested appearance. The results are temporary and will last for between three and six months. Usually patients have several injections over a period of a year or two, but as muscles lose the habit of frowning or wrinkling, the need for treatment is reduced.

It's important to choose an experienced consultant as too much botox can leave you looking flat or expressionless. There is also a 1–2 per cent risk of brow and eyelid ptosis, or drooping. This is temporary, lasting no longer than two weeks, and the risk can be minimized by strictly following the aftercare instructions. Price: £250–£350.

Fillers

Over the years, muscle and tissue begin to sag and lips lose their plumpness through natural wear and tear, lines and wrinkles form and cheeks hollow – all helping to give a tired, drawn, rather sad appearance. Injectable fillers can be used to remove wrinkles and folds, firm facial contours and replump the lips and cheeks. They are used particularly to treat frown lines, nasolabial folds (the lines that run from nose to mouth), thinning or shapeless lips, down-turning mouths, and perioral, or smoker's, lines. There are several different types of filler readily available now.

Collagen injections These were the first fillers on the market and are still the best known. It's a short, easy procedure lasting only about 30 minutes, but there are side effects. Because the solution is derived from human and animal sources, for instance bovine collagen, there have been cases of allergic reactions. You've only got to look at the pictures of the actress Leslie Ash to see what can go wrong. The effects are also very short-lived and repeat injections are needed after six months. Collagen fillers are rarely used now due to the problems with allergic reactions. Price: from £200.

Hyaluronic fillers This is now the most popular group of fillers. They are free from animal products and derived from a natural polysaccharide that breaks down naturally over time, so there's much less chance of an allergic reaction. Two of the most effective are **Restylane** and **Perlane**, which are often used for deep folds, thinning lips, lip lines and facial firming and contouring. They will also treat acne scars. Both Restylane and Perlane last well, roughly twice as long as collagen – six to nine months is common and 12 months is not unusual, after which a top-up treatment will be required. Price: from £300.

Isolagen This new treatment involves injecting yourself with your own skin cells to boost your collagen production. A small tissue sample taken from behind your ear is sent to a lab, where it's used to grow millions of fibroblasts (cells that produce collagen). This takes about eight weeks. These new cells are then injected back into the areas you want to treat to speed up cell production, fill out wrinkles and give your skin a new elasticity and firmness. The improvements last for 18 to 24 months and so far results have been very successful for 92 per cent of people. Results do depend on your cells' natural collagen-producing activity, which obviously slows with age. Price: from £2,500.

Fat transfer Fat cells are taken from one part of your body, usually the hips, buttocks or thighs, and injected back into other parts to fill out deep lines and wrinkles. This procedure is most often used to fill out sunken cheeks, deep folds around the mouth and eyes, and can also be used to create fuller lips and soften sharp chins. It lasts longest in the more static areas of the face. Fat transfer is a more complicated procedure than other fillers, and recovery time is usually a week to 10 days. Results vary, but should last three to six months, with some patients reporting improvements for a year or more. Price: from £500.

With the use of all filler injections there is some danger of infection. There can also be redness, swelling, tenderness and itching in the treated area. Patients who suffer from cold sores may find that any injections to their lips cause an outbreak, so they should speak to their doctor about a prescription for anti-viral medicine to counteract this.

DID YOU KNOW?
You must remain upright (no bending or lying down) for three to four hours after botox injections, and you shouldn't fly for 24 hours after treatment.

Chemical peels

These are used to improve the texture and appearance of the skin and to treat signs of ageing such as wrinkles, sun damage and blemishes, and skin problems such as acne. A facial peel is one of the few cosmetic procedures that actually stimulates the production of collagen in the skin.

The most effective is the medium peel which consists of 70 per cent glycolic acid, but this is quite an intense peel. At first skin looks as if it has severe sunburn, then it starts to peel after two or three days. The length of time it takes to peel totally and recover depends on the depth of the peel. The effects last for about a year and the treatment shouldn't be performed more than once a year. Price: from £100.

Lighter peels are also available, where the level of peeling is so slight that you won't even notice it. These are more suitable for people who are just starting to show some signs of ageing.

Micro-dermabrasion

This procedure uses minute crystals to scrub or scrape away surface imperfections on your skin. It's particularly useful for fine lines and acne scarring. It also stimulates the skin to produce more collagen, leaving it tightened and smooth. Fresh skin begins to appear after about two weeks, but until then treated areas will be red, sore and often crusty and flaky. You won't see full results for at least two months. A maintenance treatment is recommended after six months. Price: £500 for a course.

Thread-vein treatment

There are two main ways of treating the red spider veins or broken capillaries that appear with age. One is Intense Pulsed Light, which is detailed on page 52, the other is Sclerotherapy, where veins are individually injected. Results can be permanent, but it won't stop new veins appearing. Most patients need at least three treatments, and often more. Price: £150 per session.

Age-defying surgery

You've thought long and hard and drastic action is called for. What options are available?

Neck lift

Fantastic for tightening the skin around the neck and lower cheek area. Incisions are made in the creases around the ears and the skin is pulled tighter to smooth out lines. It's very effective for anyone with loose, turkey-style skin under the chin. The operation usually takes about two hours and involves an overnight stay. Average recovery time is three to four weeks but scarring may not fade for up to two years. Scars will be pink and defined for at least six weeks and sometimes do not change very much for some months. Price: from £3,500.

Neck liposuction

An incision is made under the chin and fat is sucked out to firm the contours of the face, improve the jawline and remove jowls. It may be combined with a chin implant to resculpt. The procedure isn't always successful; it just doesn't work on some people. If you have thin, loose skin, you can be left with sagging, excess flesh. The older or heavier you are, the less likely your skin is to spring back into shape. Price: from £1,500.

Laser skin resurfacing

A laser passes over your face, burning the skin in small, circular movements. It smoothes the skin significantly and treats fine lines around the mouth, eyes and on the cheeks. This is quite a deep, aggressive procedure, requiring a local anaesthetic for small areas, and a general anaesthetic for all-over facial treatment. Skin can look very red for one to three months, there may be some swelling and there can be a change in skin pigmentation. Price: from £2,500 per treatment.

Rhinoplasty or nose job

A prominent nose can be ageing, and noses can appear bigger as your face thins and skin sags. During surgery, the cartilage and bone are filed to reshape the bridge of the nose, which is usually broken in four places. The cartilage around the nostrils can be moved to reshape the tip. Scarring varies according to the extent of the surgery, and it can take up to three months for all the swelling to go down. If the procedure can be carried out internally, there may be no scarring. Price: £2,000–3,000.

> **DID YOU KNOW?**
> Cosmetic acupuncture and homeopathy can help reduce bruising and speed healing after surgery.

DID YOU KNOW?

It is recommended that you sleep sitting up for 14 days after face-lift surgery. » For procedures such as upper, lower or full face lifts, you must give up smoking for two weeks before and two weeks after surgery to avoid complications. Smoking also increases recovery time.

Blepharoplasty or eye-bag removal

For upper-eye surgery, excess skin and fat are removed from the eyelids and surrounding area; the scar runs along the crease of the eyelid. With under-eye surgery (or subconjunctival blepharoplasty) there is no scar as the incision is made inside the lower eyelid. Fat is taken from under the muscle and the inner corner of the eye. This procedure boasts some of the best results for hidden scarring, but complications can include dry eyes caused by tear duct damage, and if too much skin is removed it can be difficult to close the eyes properly. If you do suffer from eye bags, however, you may be comforted to know that there is nothing you could have done to prevent them as they are genetic and the only solution is surgery. Price: £2,000–£5,000.

Brow lift

As we age, our brows drop, making us look as if we're permanently frowning. A brow lift literally lifts the skin on the forehead, and sometimes the muscles beneath, to make them tighter. If done subtly, this can create a more youthful, softer face and stop your permanent relaxed expression being a frown.

If done badly, you'll look permanently startled. Keyhole surgery using an endoscope means only a few tiny staples or studs will be left about an inch into the hairline. These will either dissolve over time or be removed. After effects include bruising around the eyes, which spreads downwards onto the face, but this usually clears in about seven to ten days. Price: from £1,500.

Face lift

Loosened skin and muscles on the face, neck and at the corners of the mouth are lifted and pulled back, giving a youthful, less saggy appearance. An incision is made around the back of the ear from the hairline down to the lobe, between the back of the ear and the bone behind. In a mini-face lift or S-lift, S-shaped incisions are made around the ears, halving the length of the scars.

A good face lift can take years off you and no one will be able to put their finger on why you look so damn good. But … this is a complicated operation and side effects can include injury to the facial nerves and blood clots. As always, it's vital to choose a good, experienced surgeon to reduce the risks and also to avoid looking over-tightened and surprised. Price: from £4,000 for a mini-lift and £6,000+ for a full face lift.

COSMETIC SURGERY PROBLEMS AND SOLUTIONS

Problem	Cause	Solution	Cost
Nose to lip lines	Laughter, smoking, genetically-inherited trait	Fillers such as Restylane/Perlane	£300+
Thin lips	Normal ageing, accelerated by smoking	Restylane/Perlane	£300+
Crow's feet	Laughter, frowning, squinting, sun damage, smoking	Botox Skin peel Laser skin resurfacing	£250–£350 £50–£100 £2,500+
Forehead lines	Wrinkling brow, frowning	Botox Brow lift	£250–£350 £1,500+
Red spider veins	Extremes of temperature, alcohol, sun	Sclerotherapy IPL	£150 £100
Wrinkles around lips	Smoking	Restylane/Perlane Skin peel	£300+ £50–£100
Uneven skin tone and pigmentation	Sun exposure	Skin peel Micro-dermabrasion	£50–£100 £500
Hollow cheeks	Smoking, general loss of elasticity	Fat transfer Restylane/Perlane	£500+ £300+
Double chin/jowls/ sagging neck	Loss of elasticity in skin	Fat transfer Liposuction Fillers Neck lift	£500+ £1,500+ £300+ £3,500+
Loose skin, generally tired, haggard appearance	General ageing, genetic traits	Face lift	£4,000+
Baggy eyes	Lack of sleep/stress/lifestyle	Botox Eye-bag removal	£250–£350 £2,000–£5,000

FACIAL HAIR

This is one of the last remaining taboos, and few women are happy to discuss the problem or admit to having it, even though it's actually very common.

Hormonal changes from the mid-30s onwards mean many women experience an increase in unwanted facial hair, particularly on the upper lip, chin and sides of the face. As you get older, some of these hairs can become quite coarse.

HAIR FACTS

⋯▷ The pattern of hair growth and the number of follicles are already determined at birth and dependent on inherited factors

⋯▷ No new hair follicles develop after you are born

⋯▷ If a hair and its follicle are totally removed, it cannot regrow

⋯▷ At least 25 per cent of middle-aged women have unwanted facial hair

⋯▷ Women have the same number of hairs on their faces and bodies as men

⋯▷ Testosterone makes hairs grow thicker, darker and longer in men, so they're just more noticeable

⋯▷ The amount of darker, coarser hair increases in all women with age

⋯▷ Increased facial hair just before and after the menopause is quite common, mainly caused by a decrease in oestrogen levels

The good news is that this is one sign of ageing you don't have to put up with. There are several options for removal.

Tweezers Great for eyebrows, but not for the rest of the face, as they can cause irritation and scarring.

Depilatory creams These work by dissolving the hair at the follicle. They work best on the body as they can irritate the more delicate skin of the face and leave hairs behind. Results usually last from two to three weeks.

Waxing This works best on the upper lip and sides of the face. It's not particularly effective for the coarser hair on the chin. It can cause discoloration on darker skins, and may leave skin irritated and swollen. There are home wax kits available, but most people opt for a salon treatment. Results last from two to six weeks.

Electrolysis Low-level electricity kills the hair follicles. Results last longer than waxing and creams, but it is time-consuming and expensive. It must be done by an expert as if it's badly performed, it can result in scarring. It works best for small areas of hair and on blonde or white hair.

Laser hair removal This is great for fair skin and dark hair but not so good for blonde or white hair. It cannot be used around the eyes. You should always consult a dermatologist before going ahead with this procedure, and it must be performed by an experienced doctor, nurse or licensed aesthetician. The treatment is slightly painful and is not as permanent as you might think. After three treatments six weeks apart, there's usually a 50–70 per cent reduction in hair. Follow-up treatments are usually necessary.

Bleaching Home bleaching kits can be used to bleach hair on the face. These are usually quite effective at reducing the appearance of the hair.

TEETH

As you get older your teeth begin to discolour and wear down. This affects the shape of your face as the lower third of your face shifts closer together. Discoloured, short teeth can age a face drastically. While filming *10 Years Younger* I met cosmetic dentist Dr Surinder Hundle and he explained what happens.

As you age, your teeth develop 'halo' shapes, which form at the edge of the tooth and become very discoloured, making teeth look older. Smoking, drinking red wine, tea and coffee, and eating dark-coloured foods all discolour teeth.

As you age . . .

⋯⋙ Teeth become dull in appearance.
⋯⋙ Your smile disappears.
⋯⋙ Gums shrink and lose their shape.
⋯⋙ Receding gums contribute to a long-in-the-tooth appearance.
⋯⋙ Gums are prone to puffiness and bleeding, leading to bad breath.
⋯⋙ Lips are also affected, especially if you're a smoker, as puckered lines appear around the mouth and at the corners.

US anti-ageing guru Dr Michael Roizen advises that flossing your teeth nightly can make a significant difference to how fast you age. He claims you can take more than six years off your age by regular flossing. This is because the bacteria that cause gum disease seem to trigger an immune response in the body that results in inflammation, including inflammation of the arteries. A recent study in Sweden backs this theory, confirming a link between gum disease and cardiovascular disease – the number one cause of premature death in the UK – in women.

Dr Hundle's simple steps to prevent and delay the effects of ageing

┈┈⇥ Brush regularly, twice a day, using a fluoride toothpaste. This helps prevent the build-up of plaque on the surface of your teeth.

┈┈⇥ Toothpaste should always contain fluoride and be non-abrasive.

┈┈⇥ Daily flossing improves plaque control and removes food debris from the areas in between your teeth, where your toothbrush can't reach.

┈┈⇥ Change your toothbrush when the bristles become splayed or worn. This is usually after three months' use.

┈┈⇥ Whether electric or manual, toothbrushes should have medium- or soft-textured bristles and a small head.

┈┈⇥ Ideally, brush teeth for two minutes with an electric toothbrush or three minutes manually.

┈┈⇥ Brush your teeth for two minutes 20 minutes after meals to allow your mouth's pH to return to normal.

┈┈⇥ When using a mouthwash, try to choose one that's alcohol-free and contains fluoride.

┈┈⇥ Visit a dental hygienist regularly, ideally every three to four months, for an oral hygiene assessment and scaling.

┈┈⇥ Visit your dentist every six months to maintain optimum dental health and identify any problems.

┈┈⇥ Maintain a healthy, balanced diet and limit sugary, acidic foods to mealtimes only.

┈┈⇥ Look after your general health and well-being.

DID YOU KNOW?
Flossing your teeth can take years off your age.

Cosmetic dentistry

Veneers, bleaching and stain removal can all make your teeth look younger and healthier and give you a gleaming starlet's smile.

Whitening

There are three main methods for teeth whitening: using trays designed by your dentist to sit snugly over your teeth which you take home to use at night; whitening with a light or laser at the dentist's surgery; or DIY home bleaching kits from a chemist.

The tray method The British Dental Health Federation recommends this method. It's the one that's been around longest and has had most research done on side effects. The dentist takes an impression of a patient's teeth to produce a custom-made tray. At home, the patient pours hydrogen peroxide gel into the tray and uses it every night for two weeks. If used correctly you can expect results that will last three years. Price: £200–£500.

Light or laser power whitening Lips and gums are coated in silicon for protection. A concentrated bleaching gel is applied to your teeth and a high-intensity light is shone onto them for an hour. The heat activates the peroxide, which penetrates the enamel and draws out the stains. The effects are similar to the take-home tray method (see below left) and last about three years. Price: £450–£700.

DIY home bleaching kits These use the same basic tray method, but the tray is a standard size and not moulded to your teeth. Results are generally not very good as the concentration of bleaching hydrogen peroxide allowed by law is so weak it has little effect. The gel can also leak from the badly fitting tray, causing mouth ulcers. Price: from £10.

Veneers

Tailor-made porcelain covers are fitted onto teeth to alter their size, shape and colour. Veneers can disguise gaps and crooked teeth and even widen smiles. A thin layer of enamel is filed from the front of the teeth and the veneers glued in place. Veneers can add bulk to the teeth, plumping out the face. They last for 10–15 years and new ones can be fitted easily. However, it's very expensive and some dentists argue that it's invasive and may even weaken teeth. Price: £400–£1,500 per tooth.

DID YOU KNOW?
Cosmetic dentistry is not taught at dental school. It's up to dentists to take courses after graduation, so always thoroughly research your dentist. » One session of power whitening is as bad for teeth as drinking half a can of fizzy drink.

EYES

I have worn glasses since I was a child and now they're a part of me. Fortunately I enjoy wearing them, which is just as well because contact lenses aren't an option for me. But there's no doubt that for some people glasses can be very ageing or, perhaps more importantly, they can make you *feel* old. If that's the case, it may be worth considering corrective eye surgery.

Laser eye surgery

This is a safe, fast and effective way to correct vision. It's suitable for most people who wear glasses or contact lenses, as long as your vision hasn't changed for two years and there's no underlying eye disease.

The latest treatment is called LASIK and it combines micro-surgery with lasers. A special instrument cuts a thin flap in the cornea, which is then lifted while the laser removes a small amount of tissue. The flap is then replaced and the cornea goes back to normal.

Recovery is usually fast, you can see immediately afterwards – some people even return to work the next day, although rest at home for two to three days is preferable. The success rate stands at 95 per cent, though if patients have a high prescription they may still need glasses or contact lenses when particularly sharp sight is required. As with all surgery, it's crucial to find a qualified, experienced practitioner. Price: from £850 per eye.

hair

When it comes to looking and feeling good, few things about your appearance are more important than your hair. Think how many times a day you check your hair in the mirror, or even in a shop window as you pass by. When you step inside a changing room to try something on, what's the first thing you do? Odds are you smooth your hair or pull out your comb . The way our hair feels affects our mood and confidence, and every woman, and probably most men, knows exactly what it means to have a 'bad hair day'.

Our hair is intimately tied up with our sexuality. Studies of human behaviour show that if an attractive member of the opposite sex walks towards us, 90 per cent of people will touch their hair. When couples separate, almost the first thing they each do is rush off to the hairdresser, often changing the style or colour they've worn for years.

If the wrong hairstyle can add 10 years to the way you look, the right one can achieve the opposite.

HAIR FACTS

---> Women's scalp hair grows faster than men's – on average 0.02 mm more per day

---> Hair is 97 per cent protein; the other 3 per cent is made up of minerals and trace elements

---> Each hair follicle grows about 20 hairs in a lifetime

---> The lifespan of a hair is between 16 months and seven years – three years is average

---> Hair can reach over a metre in length

---> Pulling a hair from its follicle stimulates the next hair to grow

---> Hair usually grows just over a centimetre a month

---> The growth and loss of hairs from each follicle are finely controlled, but don't happen at the same time as other follicles, otherwise everyone would go temporarily bald

---> Hair grows more slowly in cold weather because circulation is more sluggish

DID YOU KNOW?
Blondes have more hairs than brunettes – probably because the individual hairs are finer – and redheads have the fewest. On an average head, blondes have 120,000 hairs, brunettes have 100,000 hairs and redheads have 90,000. » The number of scalp hairs also varies with ethnicity. Black people have roughly 108,000 hairs, while Asians can have as few as 80,000.

Hair facts as you age

Up to your 20s

⇢ You are born with an average of 1,100 hair follicles per square centimetre.

⇢ Hair grows fastest from the age of 16 to 24.

⇢ Children's hair grows at a rate of up to 0.41 mm per day.

⇢ The number of hair follicles is determined genetically by the time you're born.

⇢ No new hair follicles develop after birth, so if a follicle is removed, it will not be replaced.

In your 20s

⇢ Your hair is thickest when you're 20.

⇢ If you have light-coloured hair, you may notice it becoming darker.

⇢ The number of follicles on the average head has dropped to 600 per square centimetre.

⇢ 20 per cent of men in their 20s experience male pattern baldness.

⇢ Your oil glands are still producing plenty of oil.

In your 30s

⇢ 40 per cent of men have noticeable hair loss by the age of 35.

⇢ The first few grey hairs begin to appear.

⇢ Hair begins to get finer.

⇢ Less oil is produced and hair needs more protection from damage.

In your 40s

⇢ There are lots more grey hairs. As we age, pigment fades and we produce less melanin.

⇢ Grey hairs are a different texture and tend to be coarser and more wiry.

⇢ Male pattern baldness becomes more obvious.

⇢ In women, oestrogen levels begin to fall, leading to thinning, drier hair.

⇢ You can lose up to 25 per cent of your hair before the loss becomes noticeable.

Your 50s and beyond

⇢ Hair continues to thin for men and women.

⇢ As we age, the number of follicles capable of growing hairs gradually declines.

⇢ Some follicles begin producing only very fine, non-pigmented hairs.

⇢ By the age of 50, the average number of hairs per square centimetre falls to 250–300 hairs.

⇢ 50 per cent of 50-year-old women have thinning hair due to falling oestrogen and rising testosterone levels.

⇢ 65 per cent of men are balding by the age of 60.

⇢ If you've reached 60 without any obvious hair loss, you will probably avoid it altogether.

⇢ Hair growth slows to roughly 0.32 mm a day.

⇢ Hair is now much drier as oil glands have really slowed production.

⇢ In your 60s grey hair tends to turn white as pigment in the hair is lost.

Hair loss

Hair naturally thins as part of the ageing process. You just have to compare the figures – the average 20-year-old has 600 hairs per square centimetre on their head, and the average 50-year-old has less than half that number. Hair loss is generally less of a problem for women because their hair tends to decrease evenly over the scalp, resulting in thinner hair rather than distinct bald patches.

DID YOU KNOW?

You lose more hair in the autumn and spring as a natural response to the changes in season and amount of daylight. » Male pattern baldness is triggered by falling levels of the hormone testosterone when it is converted to dihydrotestosterone. This is at least partly genetically predetermined. » It's quite normal to lose 100–125 scalp hairs a day. » A straight parting will draw attention to your scalp and highlight thinning, so go for a tousled look of varying lengths. Keeping hair all one length can drag hair down and make it look even thinner.

Causes of hair loss

⋯⟩ **Pregnancy and the Pill** Hormonal changes can cause hair loss, but this is virtually always temporary. It's important to be very gentle with your hair and avoid harsh products or treatments.

⋯⟩ **Smoking** This affects the body's take-up of vitamin C and constricts the blood vessels, which means fewer nutrients reach the hair to encourage growth.

⋯⟩ **Drinking** Alcohol destroys B vitamins, which are essential for healthy glossy hair.

⋯⟩ **Stress** Anxiety and stress can lead to hair problems and can even cause it to fall out. Try gentle scalp massage to stimulate the follicles.

⋯⟩ **Poor diet** Thinning hair or hair loss can be associated with a lack of iron, B and C vitamins and lysine. Try to boost your diet and include plenty of water and essential fatty acids.

⋯⟩ **Perming, bleaching or dyeing** If constantly over-treated, hair can become brittle and break off close to the scalp. Seek professional advice from a reputable hair salon.

Hair care

Healthy, thick, shiny hair is definitely associated with youth, and, like your face, your hair needs looking after.

There is a huge variety of products to choose from, and it's worth shopping around and varying the shampoos and conditioners you use. With hair care, a change really can be as good as a rest. Look at what's available and choose something to match your hair type.

Shampoos

---> Don't wash hair more than once a day as you will strip away all the natural protection that helps to make it look thick and shiny.

---> If your hair is coloured or permed, a specially formulated shampoo will gently cleanse it and won't strip the colour out.

---> Volumizing shampoos contain proteins that bond with your hair. Avoid using them all the time as they can leave a residue, which builds up, making hair look dull and dragging it down.

---> Highlight-enhancing shampoos and conditioners can make grey hair look shiny and help avoid the yellow tint that grey hair can sometimes acquire.

---> Acidic, clarifying shampoos containing ingredients such as lemon juice or vinegar help to strip away the residue that builds up from your normal hair products. These are ideal to use before applying an intense conditioner or before a salon treatment as they will help it work better.

---> It used to be a common myth that washing your hair too often would make it oily or unhealthy. Leading trichologists now argue the opposite – the best thing you can do for your hair is make sure it is clean and conditioned, shampooing every day if necessary. You will know what works best for you and certainly if you have long, dry hair, every other day, or even every two days, may be better.

DID YOU KNOW?

As a rule of thumb, your hair will need more frequent shampooing and a lighter conditioner in the summer, when the heat can increase sweat production and make your scalp greasier. » Sunlight fades natural and applied colour, and is very drying. It's a good idea to condition your hair using a leave-in conditioner with a UV filter for protection.

Conditioners

Leave-in conditioners can work well on dry hair. But as they coat your hair, they can weigh it down, making it look lifeless. Use too much and your hair can appear greasy.

Rinse-out conditioners are always my first choice. They smooth my hair and eliminate tangles, making it easier to comb and style. As long as they are well rinsed out, they won't drag your hair down either.

Deep conditioners, hair masks, waxes or oils are great occasionally. They need to be left on for at least 10 minutes to work properly, and are good for treated or dry hair, really helping to moisturize and strengthen the hair. To help the treatment penetrate deeper, wrap hair in a hot towel. Think of them in the same way as a monthly facial.

Volumizing conditioners use ingredients such as collagen, keratin and proteins to plump out individual hairs.

Combined shampoos and conditioners are a great idea, but it seems to me they neither shampoo nor condition as effectively as individual products. I'll concede that they're useful if you're travelling and want to cut down on the number of bottles you're taking, but even then I'd rather decant my usual products into small travel bottles.

You can choose different makes of shampoo and conditioner. I tend to go for the same brand as I feel they're more likely to complement each other, but it's up to you.

DID YOU KNOW?
Choose a light conditioner for fine hair – richer conditioners will just weigh it down. » If your hair snaps easily, try applying infusions of rosemary or nettle to strengthen it. » Ask your hairstylist for advice on products and the best way to maintain your style, and watch what he or she does. » Hanging upside down can improve circulation and blood flow to the scalp, stimulating hair follicles, while a gentle, invigorating scalp massage will also boost circulation and aid regrowth.

Shampooing

⇢ If your hair is unhealthy looking, check the pH balance of your shampoo as many are alkaline and will dull hair over time. Your scalp's natural pH is between 4 and 6.
⇢ Focus on the scalp area, gently massaging to stimulate the follicles, especially if the ends are dry.
⇢ For a good lather, thoroughly wet your hair first.
⇢ Many shampoos recommend washing twice, but if your hair is dry or fragile, once is probably sufficient.
⇢ If you live in a soft-water area, go easy on the amount of shampoo you use as it'll take hours to rinse out otherwise.

Conditioning

⇢ Use a small amount of conditioner.
⇢ Start at the ends and work your way up to the scalp.
⇢ Gently comb conditioner through your hair before rinsing to smooth the hair shaft.

Rinsing

⇢ Rinse for the final time with cold water. This makes the hair contract and the cuticle lie flat.
⇢ Pat wet hair with a towel – don't rub.

Feeding your hair

If your body is healthy and well nourished, your hair will reflect this and look glossy and vibrant.

For good hair health, eat a diet rich in:
⇢ Beta carotene
⇢ Essential fatty acids
⇢ Iron
⇢ Magnesium
⇢ Silica
⇢ Sulphur
⇢ Vitamins B, C, E
⇢ Zinc

From dry or oily hair to premature hair loss, many hair problems are linked to what you eat:
⇢ Oily hair can be a sign of vitamin B deficiency.
⇢ Dry, brittle hair can occur if your diet is lacking in essential fatty acids.
⇢ Poor hair growth or loss of colour are signs of zinc deficiency.
⇢ Dandruff can be caused by stress. The oil producing glands can begin overworking, causing dead cells to fall off in clumps rather than one by one. Try using a shampoo containing zinc, sulphur, tar or selenium, and boosting your dietary intake of essential minerals may also help.

Styling and drying

···⇢ Do use styling products. They add shine and texture as well as 'setting' your style.

···⇢ Choose products carefully to match your particular hair type.

···⇢ If you're unsure, talk to your hairdresser or ask for advice in a beauty store such as Space NK, where the assistants usually have a good knowledge of a range of different products.

···⇢ Don't make the mistake of using too many products at once – they may well cancel each other out and you won't know what works best.

···⇢ Less is more. You won't get a better result by slathering on the treatment. Hair will just end up looking sticky or dull. For fine or thin hair, you need even less.

···⇢ Choose a good-quality hairdryer. Cheaper models often rely on too much heat, which is damaging. Look for well-powered dryers between 1,200 and 2,000 watts.

···⇢ Keep the heat setting on low as far as possible.

···⇢ Don't concentrate for too long on one spot when drying your hair.

···⇢ Natural bristle brushes are best as they're gentle on the hair and reduce static. Look after them by removing hairs and washing regularly in a mild shampoo solution. Always rinse thoroughly.

···⇢ Hairspray is fantastic for keeping swept-up hairstyles in place. Just go easy and choose a light spray, as rigid, immovable hair is ageing and not very sexy.

DID YOU KNOW?

Don't delay styling your hair. The moisture in towel-dried hair helps styling products work better.》 Heat, whether from hairdryers, tongs or irons, is very drying. It literally steams the moisture from your hair and overuse will leave your hair parched and dull. 》You should always point the hairdryer down along the hair shaft – this helps to flatten the cuticles so they'll reflect the light and make your hair shinier.

Choosing a hairstyle

Over time, your face, colouring, lifestyle and persona all change, and your hairstyle needs to keep pace. There's no more instant way to update your image than a good cut and colour.

If you're going to spend money on just one thing, then I think the cut is the most important. When my hair is well cut I know it will also grow out well, making it a good investment as I'll only need to revisit my stylist once every four months. Movement and softness all come from your cut. A clever cut will emphasize your best features and draw attention away from the worst.

Try not to be swayed by what's in vogue; instead think about what suits your style, what's 'you'? Hair is intimately tied up with your image, so don't lose sight of that. Even subtle changes can be effective.

STYLING FACTS

⤏ The shape of your face changes over the years, in particular your chin and jawline become less defined. A clever haircut can help disguise this

⤏ Don't stick to the same parting. Change it and you'll be surprised at the extra bounce and body your hair has

⤏ Side partings are generally more flattering, whatever your face shape

⤏ The cold weather makes hair lie close to your scalp. This helps to keep your head warm but can make your hair look flat

Hair tricks

Hair can be very useful for camouflaging some of the more obvious signs of ageing:

Frown lines Have a fringe cut – this can be soft or full, depending on your face shape, and it doesn't need to be short. Just a few curls or wispy tendrils can do the trick.

Crow's feet Frame your face with a cut that naturally falls softly forward around the sides, and avoid pulling hair sharply back from your face.

Sagging jaw Try soft waves around the jawline, or a feathered cut that's a little shaggy around the jaw. You can draw attention away from your chin and jaw with more detail at the crown.

Round face Bring hair forward around the cheeks to camouflage your lack of cheekbone definition, and go for a layered cut rather than a bob.

FRINGE FACTS

- A heavy fringe works best on narrow, oval faces as it can make your face look wider

- A fringe is a good way to shorten long faces

- Lighter, textured fringes that can be swept to one side are more flattering for rounder, heart-shaped faces

- Keep long fringes straight and kink-free with a straightening iron

- Fringes can make you look younger, but before you rush off to the hairdresser, make sure it will suit your face

My top tips for youthful locks

⋯⋗ Avoid severe, blunt cuts as you get older. Short, geometric hairstyles can make an older face look harsh and rough.

⋯⋗ Don't assume you need to cut off your hair – shoulder-length or even slightly longer hair can be very flattering as long as it's kept in good condition. It's a myth that you must have short hair as you age.

⋯⋗ Go for soft rather than tight curls, and vary the curl size.

⋯⋗ Unless you intend to work very hard at your make-up, don't pull your hair back tightly from your face. It's a sure way to add years to your look and will draw attention to every wrinkle and flaw.

⋯⋗ Use hair to soften your face and hide your wrinkles.

⋯⋗ Stiff, rigid hairstyles and too much hairspray will leave hair looking unnatural and make you look a decade older.

⋯⋗ Childish hair ties, bobbles and scrunchies are a mistake. They will make you look frumpy and only serve to emphasize your age.

TIP

You don't have to play safe with your haircut and colour just because you're getting older. Be bold – you might get a pleasant surprise. On the other hand, subtle changes can be just as effective in updating your look. The key is to go with what you want, what suits you and what makes you feel most confident.

Colour

How soon you begin to go grey and the rate at which your hair changes colour are largely results of your genes. A few people will notice the odd grey hair before their 21st birthday, while others never go grey at all.

External factors, such as stress and a diet lacking in essential nutrients, can all accelerate the process, but whatever the underlying cause, there's no doubt that grey hair is intimately wrapped up with the idea of ageing. But it's not just the colour, as one of my clients recently complained, it's the coarse, wiry texture that's the real shock.

When considering hair colour, you must always take into account your natural skin tone and eye colour. Your underlying tone will either be warm or cool, whatever your nationality, and it's always most flattering to choose a hair colour that complements it.

Top hairstylist Beverley Cobella explains that many women make the mistake of thinking hair colour should be darker as they get older. In fact the reverse is true. You lose melanin (pigment) from the skin as you age, so your skin colour changes and lightens. To complement this, hair colour should also be lighter, and it's much more flattering to opt for a warmer tone. Two or three different colours give the best effect – even blonde hair shouldn't be just one shade but a mixture, with darker tones underneath to add texture, life and movement, all of which help create a younger image. The idea is to improve on nature, and no one's hair is ever naturally one single colour.

How will you grey?

Your natural colour	Shade of grey
Black	Steel grey
Dark brown	Steel grey
Light brown	Mousy grey
Blonde	Mousy grey
Auburn/red	Faded red

Choosing a colour

There's no substitute for finding a good colourist, who will advise you on the colours and shades that work best for you. Skilful use of colour can make hair look thicker, glossier and really help you roll back the years to appear younger and sexier. On the opposite page are some general guidelines that can be useful when you're thinking about a change, but haven't got as far as the salon.

DID YOU KNOW?
Dark hair shades can emphasize lines and make skin look older, making lighter shades a better option as you age, but don't go too far as too light is also ageing. » Black and peroxide blonde are both very difficult colours to wear and often aren't flattering; you need lots of make-up to balance the effect. » Choose warmer hair tones to give you a youthful glow. » Sun, sea and chlorine all rob hair of colour, so reintroduce some depth to your colour in the autumn. » Dyed, straightened or permed hair is more porous and will absorb colour faster, so always tell your colourist if you've had any hair treatments. » Highlights or a vegetable colour will add gloss to greying hair, and the resulting increased shine and movement will automatically make hair appear more youthful.

COLOUR CHART

Your eye colour	Possible hair colours to consider
Dark brown	Dark auburn, copper, coppery blonde
Light brown	Dark auburn, bronze/auburn, pastel blondes
Blue	Light/medium brown, dark shades of blonde, silver
Grey blue or hazel	Golden, ash blonde
Green	Reddish blonde

Complexion type	Possible hair colours to consider
Fair	Blonde, auburn, ash blonde (most colours can look good, apart from very dark)
Rosy	Ash blonde, brown, ash brown. Avoid reds and warm gold
Olive	Deep auburn, mahogany. Totally avoid light/bright shades
Sallow	Copper, auburn (which helps your skin glow), beige blonde. Avoid dark shades and gold
Dark brown/black	Warm dark shades, rich and subtle highlights on dark hair

And if you must go blonde	Possible shades to consider
Fair	Soft ash blonde
Rosy	Deeper ash blonde
Olive	Avoid medium to deep beige tones
Sallow	Warm beige

Hair extensions

Long, lustrous hair is often associated with youth, and certainly growing hair takes patience and lots of hard work, especially when the years are conspiring to slow down the speed of growth and thin out what's there. Take a leaf out of Victoria Beckham's book and cheat – hair extensions are a readily available option. They take time and they're certainly not cheap, but when put in by an expert they're extremely effective. They last roughly three months, after which you may well want to go back for more. Human hair extensions cost from £150 for extra volume to thicken hair and from £500 if you want to add length.

Extension facts

⋯⇢ Hair must be at least 8 cm long to have extensions attached.

⋯⇢ If you want to colour or perm your hair, it must be done before the extensions are attached, then the new hair is chosen to match.

⋯⇢ You can opt for real human hair, synthetic fibre or even horse hair. Human hair is the most effective and also the most expensive.

⋯⇢ Batches of 20–30 strands are usually bonded to your own hair close to the scalp.

⋯⇢ Once attached, hair is cut to shape and styled. It's important to keep your new hair clean as grease can wear down the resin bond holding the extensions in place. You also have to be careful about brushing, but bad hair days should become a thing of the past.

Wefts

If the thought of extensions doesn't appeal, wefts are another option. They have long been used by supermodels and are now available in most salons . A weft is a piece of human hair with a couple of clips on it. You simply clip the weft into your own hair when you're after a more glamorous look for a night out. Wefts cost between £50 and £70 each and are usually dyed to the colour of your hair, or can even be a different colour, depending on the look you're trying to achieve. A must-have accessory!

Black hair

Tight braiding over a long period of time can result in pressure on the follicles, especially around the hairline. This can eventually lead to scar tissue forming in the follicle, meaning that the hair will stop growing altogether.

There is now quite a range of products specially developed to treat the scalp, stimulating cell and keratin production and improving circulation to the hair root. Look out for repair treatments to moisturize fragile, damaged or chemically treated hair, restoring strength and shine. For specialist knowledge it's worth contacting The Institute of Trichologists (see the Directory on page 280).

Relaxing hair

Both relaxing and colouring products contain strong chemicals so you should wait two weeks between using them. Watch out for new products from a US company called Luster, soon to be available here, which include a relaxer and colourant in one. Ask your hairdresser for advice.

Colour treatments

It's vital to keep hair hydrated, using weekly deep-conditioning products and leave-in conditioners to lock in colour and protect your hair.

Weaves

These can work well if you want to give your hair a rest or try an instant new style. There are two main types – cornrow based or bonded.

Cornrow New hair, which can be either human or synthetic, is sewn onto a cornrow. When done well, the cornrows can give the impression of a natural parting in the hair.

Bonded Weaves are either hot- or cold-sealed onto your natural hair.

Both types of weave need specific care and it's advisable to speak to your stylist about the best products to use. Weaves cost from £100 for the first fitting and styling. If you compare that with the cost of chemical treatments and relaxing, the price isn't very high.

DID YOU KNOW?
Weaves should not be left in for more than three months. After the weave has been removed your natural hair will need a specialist moisturizing and conditioning salon treatment. If you want to go on using weaves, you will have to replace the hair every three months.

beauty

CHAPTER FOUR

If you've had the same make-up routine for as long as you can remember, and your make-up bag is bulging with half-used pots and samples, it's definitely time for a change and a make-up MOT. Trust me, it's not painful and it's an easy way to lose years and update a frumpy image.

It's important to learn the tricks of the trade, but as you get older, less is usually more, and every product you use will have a job to do. The right application makes all the difference – badly applied make-up looks trashy and ageing.

DID YOU KNOW?
Book an appointment with a make-up artist or beauty-counter consultant for some make-up advice. She will be able to recommend products and show you how to use them properly. It's worth going once every couple of years to find out what's new, and there's no better way of ensuring you don't get stuck in a make-up rut. » Always moisturize at least half an hour before applying make-up to allow the cream to be absorbed. This will prevent your make-up sliding and will help it last longer.

Make-up bag MOT

Throw away

⋯⟶ Messy tubes and compacts
⋯⟶ Anything that's broken or squashed
⋯⟶ All those samples you've never used
⋯⟶ Everything you haven't worn for the past year
⋯⟶ Brushes that are losing their bristles
⋯⟶ Sponges that look as if they've been eaten
⋯⟶ Liquids that are separating
⋯⟶ Mascaras that are more than a few months old
⋯⟶ Everything that smells odd
⋯⟶ Check the bag itself. Does it just need a clean
or are you due for a new one?

Believe me, you'll feel so much better and more organized afterwards. The chances are you only ever used less than 10 per cent of the contents.

> TIP
> **Select a mini make-up kit to take out with you. Multi-function products are a fantastic way to reduce the amount of make-up you need to carry around.**

Foundation

Skin becomes drier with the years, and signs of ageing such as spider veins, dark shadows and the odd wrinkle all make foundation an essential for youthful, dewy skin.

Beware, however, of wearing too much foundation, as it can be ageing. The more you try to hide your wrinkles, the more obvious they can become. You should look for a high-pigment, light-textured foundation that will cover blemishes but appear light and luminous on the skin.

Always choose a colour foundation that matches your skin tone exactly. Ask a beauty counter assistant for advice. It's best to try products on your jawline – it's an urban myth that you should try them out on the inside of your wrist as the skin there is usually a completely different colour from that on your face. Ranges like Prescriptives will actually mix a foundation specifically to match your skin.

Use a light-textured foundation only where you need it. If you've chosen a shade that matches your skin well, you won't have to smooth it on everywhere. Remember that youthful skin is fresh and clear and that's what you should aim for. The more natural your make-up, the more youthful you'll appear.

I always apply foundation with my fingers as I achieve a better result, but you can use brushes or a damp sponge. Go for whatever works for you. There's no one right way, but try to pat foundation *into* your skin rather than dragging it across.

Powder

Powder can be useful to set your make-up, especially if you have oily skin or are prone to a shiny face. It will also help to protect your skin and lock in moisture, which is always important, even for oily skins.

Always apply powder by patting it down onto the skin instead of wiping it across your face. You can use a brush, puff or sponge. Experiment to find out what works for you. I have to say I never use powder as it's not necessary to set foundation and it can take away your natural glow and make you look older.

DID YOU KNOW?
If your skin is very dry, pat on a little rich moisturizer after applying your foundation to make your skin look fresher. I'm assuming, of course, that you've already thoroughly cleansed and moisturized your face first. » Go easy with the face powder or you'll find it settles in all the wrinkles you'd really rather hide. » If your pores tend to be large, finger-applied foundation is more effective than a sponge, which tends to deposit too much, visibly clogging pores. » Avoid foundation or blusher containing iridescence, sparkles or glitter. It's very ageing on any but the youngest faces.

Concealer

Concealers should also match your skin tone, and less is definitely more. Hide those blemishes and red veins, but don't make your skin look caked and unnatural.

Light-diffusing concealers work well to hide dark under-eye shadows. Peachy or yellow undertones will help hide blue shadows and make it look like you've had a full eight hours' sleep. The texture is also important. Opt for one that feels smooth and light. Concealer should glide over any lines rather than settling into them. Again, you can apply with a brush or fingertips – go with whatever works for you.

A good concealer should be:
- Smooth, light and creamy.
- The colour should blend easily with your skin.
- It should have peachy or yellow undertones.

A good concealer should never be:
- Greasy, chalky, sticky or dry.
- It should not have white or pink undertones.
- It should never be lighter than your skin.

Blusher

Blusher works wonders for pale, pasty faces, and even those with more natural colour can benefit from the definition it adds to cheekbones.

The choice of cream or powder is all down to personal preference. If you go for a powder, I would strongly recommend using a brush, as you'll get a much smoother effect. Avoid anything greasy as the colour will streak, looking unnatural and uneven.

Apply blusher lightly to the apples of your cheeks and under the cheekbones to sculpt your face. As a guide, suck in your cheeks to find the hollows, and blend outwards towards the hairline. Use circular sweeping movements and blend the colour away to almost nothing. You're aiming for definition and warmth.

TIPS

Don't skimp on foundation and concealers. They provide your base and the better quality they are, the better the results. If you get your foundation right, your make-up will look fresher and more youthful. » If your skin is dry, try using a foundation primer. » Never opt for a concealer that is a lighter tone than your skin – it will instantly add a decade to your age. » To cover sun spots and uneven pigmentation, blend concealer and foundation together. If you're applying them separately, always apply foundation before concealer.

Lips

Lips tend to thin and lose colour as we get older, but you don't have to resort to fillers and injections to make them appear fuller.

Lip tips

---> Buff your lips gently using a cotton bud soaked in eye make-up remover to slough off any dead skin.

---> Use a conditioning lip balm to moisturize your lips rather than a product that's just protective.

---> Use a fine lip brush or lip liner to outline your lips. Draw the line just outside your natural contours for a fuller look.

---> Alternatively, use concealer to draw around the edge of your lips and colour in with lip colour. This will also make your lips appear fuller.

---> Choose light to medium colours.

---> Highlight the centre of your lips or add a dab of lip gloss right in the middle to catch the light and enhance your pout.

---> If you prefer lip gloss, choose one with a rosy tone to enhance your natural lip colour.

---> Lip gloss shouldn't be applied outside your natural lip line.

---> To get a true idea of colour when choosing a new lipstick, don't try it on top of another one. There's no point in testing it on your hand as your skin colour is nothing like the colour of your lips and the lipstick will look totally different. If you really don't want to test the colour on your lips, try it on your fingertips, where the skin is closer in colour.

The perfect pout

---> Opaque, matt colours generally make lips look thinner, while shimmery shades and glosses make lips appear fuller.

---> Avoid oranges and dark purples, as they're very ageing and unflattering on most faces. Very dark shades are also difficult to apply perfectly and often come off on your teeth.

---> Emphasize either your eyes *or* your lips. Too much drama will look dated and old.

DID YOU KNOW?
Cool-toned lip colours such as red- and blue-based pinks make teeth look whiter. Avoid orange and brown tones as they will make your teeth look yellow.

Eyes

Always start with an eye cream to depuff and moisturize the delicate area around your eyes; this will give you a good base for everything else. As we age, the skin on our eyelids thins, so it's worth using a natural colour eyeshadow to give a smooth, even tone. Lighter shades will also help open up the eyes.

Choose soft, neutral eyeshadow shades with sheer textures to create smokier, younger-looking eyes. Anything too bright or shiny will be overpowering and make you look older. Shimmery eyeshadows tend to settle into any wrinkles and reflect light, therefore drawing attention to them. Matt tones are a safer, more youthful bet.

Eyebrows

As we get older our upper eyelids tend to start sagging, which closes the eye area. Plucking and shaping your eyebrows can give you an instant face lift, and really open up the eyes. Eyebrows also tend to get longer and wiry as we age, so keep them trimmed.

How to pluck

···> A good pair of tweezers is a worthwhile investment. They'll last and hurt less.

···> A tiny dab of mouth-ulcer gel can help numb eyebrows before plucking, or rub an ice cube along your brow.

···> Always grasp the hair you want to pluck as close to the skin as possible.

···> Tweeze out the hair in the direction in which it's growing but don't get carried away and pluck out too many hairs.

···> A white highlighter can help you draw in the shape you want before you pluck out the hairs.

···> To determine where your arch should be, hold a pencil at a 45-degree angle on the outer edge of your iris (the coloured part of your eye). Where the pencil touches your brow is where the arch of your brow should be.

···> If you're still unsure about the shape or arch you should go for, make an appointment with a professional and use what they do as a guide for the future.

Finish eyebrows with a subtle powder, brushed on using a brow brush rather than a pencil. This will give you a more subtle, natural effect while adding shape and definition to your brows, which is particularly important as ageing skin loses its tone.

Eyeliner

⋯⊹ Eyeliner will define and emphasize your eyes. For most people brown is a good choice and will give a softer, less harsh effect than black. But should you choose liquid liner or a soft pencil? I have to say I like both.

Liquid liner

⋯⊹ With a little practice, liquid liner is just as easy to apply and gives a more finished, dramatic look, especially for evenings out. Everyone has different techniques and preferences – some people swear by leaning an elbow on a table for steadiness, some like a fine brush, others a thicker one or sponge wand. The choice is yours and you'll need to experiment to find out what you like best, then practise.

⋯⊹ Lines should always be drawn close to the lashes, with a small flick out and upwards at the outer corner of the eye. It's often easiest to start from the middle of the eyelid, and you could try using a matching pencil to draw the line from the inner corner of your eye for a softer effect.

Eye pencil

You may prefer the softer effect you can achieve with eye pencils, especially if you have quite small eyelids. Line the entire lash line close to the lashes, and experiment with different colours and with smudging and softening the line.

Eyeshadow

You can also use eyeshadow instead of eyeliner to outline your eyes. hard edges can be ageing and a softer, more blended look can divert attention from the more obvious signs of ageing, such as crow's feet.

TIPS
If you line only the outside half of your eyes, you'll make them look smaller and more close set, so always draw eyeliner along the whole length of your eyelid.
» To brighten your eyes, cover them with cotton-wool pads soaked in witch hazel, then lie back and relax for five minutes.
» Keep a supply of cotton buds to hand when applying eye make-up. They're invaluable for correcting mistakes and softening lines. » If your eyes are fairly deep-set, avoid dark eyeshadow and choose an eyeliner to emphasize them.

Mascara

···⟩ Before applying mascara, *always* curl your eyelashes. Nothing opens your eyes more. Then sweep on mascara to complete your look. By curling your lashes first you'll also find that mascara goes on better and doesn't rub off so easily.

···⟩ Brown mascara is less ageing than black on fair skins, but if you have olive or dark skin and brown eyes, black will look more dramatic.

···⟩ There are so many types of mascaras to choose from now, but most will add either volume or length, or promise a more natural effect. Experiment – mascaras don't have to be expensive.

Perfume

Beauty is all about how you feel, and nothing lifts your mood like a gorgeous scent. Everyone's taste is different, so I'm not going to suggest what you should choose, but here are a few basics that are worth knowing.

···❯ Eau de parfum and pure perfume last longer and are more intense than eau de toilette. They're also more expensive.

···❯ Try both on your skin – what works best will depend on your skin's natural chemistry.

···❯ When choosing a new perfume, try scents on perfume cards first.

···❯ Only try the ones you like best on your skin.

···❯ It's a waste of time trying more than two different scents at once. Your nose can only cope with two before getting confused.

···❯ If you find a new perfume you like, ask for a sample and try it out for a week at home to see if you really like it. Some perfumes are great on the first whiff but get a bit toxic once you've worn them for some hours.

···❯ Apply perfume to pulse points such as the inner wrists, behind the ears and the base of the neck.

···❯ Spray perfume up into the air and walk through the falling mist to acquire a good overall scent.

'The secret of beauty is smiling and feeling good in yourself.'

SOPHIE MARCEAU, ACTRESS

My top tips for youthful beauty

---> Simple products are often better as we get older. Brasher, brighter experiments with make-up are strictly for the young.

---> Less is more – piled-on make-up is always ageing. Aim for a natural, radiant glow.

---> Choose high-pigment, light-textured foundation for a flawless, dewy look. Remember that youthful skin is fresh and clear and the more natural-looking your skin, the more youthful you'll seem.

---> Concealer can work wonders. It will hide dark shadows and eliminate age spots, but use in moderation.

---> A rosy blush will instantly add a glow to skin that's lost its colour and pigment over the years. This is particularly important in winter when skin loses its natural lustre.

---> Pluck your eyebrows. A well-shaped brow instantly lifts your face and takes 10 years off your age.

---> Emphasize your eyes *or* your lips, not both – unless you want to look older and dated.

---> Wear a natural eyeshadow to smooth your eyelids and brighten your eyes.

---> Always curl your lashes with an eyelash curler before slicking on mascara as it really opens up your eyes.

---> Choose glossy shades for lips, rather than opaque matt colours.

---> Wear perfume every day. It lifts your mood and makes you smile, as well as smelling delicious. What could be more anti-ageing?

'To feel glamorous I don't need anything but moisturized skin and red lipstick.'

SCARLETT JOHANSSON, ACTRESS

NAILS

The condition of your nails is a real indicator of your lifestyle and diet. Good nutrition will show up in pink, smooth nails. Sadly genetics and age play a part in the appearance of your nails and you may find that ridges begin to appear when you reach your 40s.

It's worth taking the time to look after your nails as they're almost always on display. Manicures are very pampering, so treat yourself to a salon appointment if you want to sit back and relax, but otherwise they're very easy to do yourself at home.

Gently scrub your nails with soapy water, rinse and dry thoroughly. Then soak your fingers in warm olive oil. It's soothing and really moisturizing.

To give hand cream an extra kick, apply it last thing at night then put on a pair of cotton gloves (or socks) and go to bed. You'll be surprised how soft your hands and feet feel in the morning.

Use almond oil instead of hand cream.

If your nails are ridged or flake a lot, run around the edges with the soft side of a nail file, then rub gently with cream or oil before you go to bed at night.

Short, well-maintained nails are always better – long talons are very ageing and trashy. The shorter your nails are, the darker the nail polish you can wear, so you can have some fun and be bold. Coordinate with your outfit if you like, or use nail polish to add a dash of colour – in the summer I like to match my toes and fingernails.

Don't dismiss pale pink or clear varnishes as boring – they can work really well and give you a chic, well-styled finish that also lasts longer. The darker the colour, the more quickly chips show up, making regular maintenance essential.

Applying polish

···⟩ Thoroughly wash and dry your hands, paying particular attention to your nails.

···⟩ File them into shape.

···⟩ Apply a base or undercoat first. This gives a good, smooth surface for polish and helps to keep the colour true. If you wear nail polish a lot, it will also stop your nails yellowing.

···⟩ Choose a conditioning product to strengthen your nails.

···⟩ Brush a stroke of polish along the centre of your nail first, painting towards the tip.

···⟩ Work outwards to the sides.

···⟩ Allow the first coat to dry before applying a second.

···⟩ A top coat adds extra gloss and protection and will help the polish last longer.

···⟩ A cotton bud dipped in nail varnish remover will neatly correct any mistakes or wobbles.

Dos and don'ts of nailcare

DO file your nails in one direction, using the less abrasive side of the emery board. DON'T saw at your nails as it weakens them. DO soak nails to soften them before gently pushing back the cuticles to reveal the white half moons. DON'T cut cuticles.

DID YOU KNOW?

White flecks can be a sign of zinc deficiency, while ridges and dryness can mean you're lacking B vitamins. They can also be a sign of general, everyday wear and tear – almost like a bruise, they show where the nail was knocked. Weak nails may simply be inherited or they can be a sign that you need more calcium.

Artificial nails

If you bite your nails or have trouble growing them, artificial nails can be a solution, and there are several different types to choose from. Remember that although artificial nails hide your own, they won't make them healthier and they can weaken them. They need regular maintenance, usually at a salon, to stop them peeling off and damaging the nail underneath.

What's available?

⇢ **Acrylic nails** These are the strongest and last the longest. The downside is that they can look very thick and false, unless you see an expert manicurist. You will normally need to see the manicurist every two or three weeks for the nails to be filled as your own nails grow.

⇢ **Gel nails** Manicurists use gel to sculpt your nail and then set it under UV light. Gel nails usually need less filling than acrylic nails but are not ideal for anyone who types a lot as this will crack the seal. Gel is porous so oxygen can reach your nail underneath. However, you should always wear gloves when using strong detergents as these can also penetrate through the pores.

⇢ **Sculptured nails** Acrylic, gel or fibreglass is applied to your own nails, then sculpted over tiny pieces of foil or metal. Another method is for a plastic nail tip to be attached and then the sculptured nail is laid over the top. As your own nails grow, the base will need to be filled and the tip filed.

⇢ **Silk, linen and fibre wraps** These are glued to the nail, adding strength and sometimes length. They can also be used with tips. Silk gives the best effect but isn't very strong. Fibreglass is probably the best choice as it is natural-looking but stronger than silk.

⇢ It's always best to have fake nails removed by a professional manicurist as this will cause the least damage to your own nails.

BEWARE
False nails always damage the nail beneath, so before you go down this route, consider cost and maintenance implications. The damage to your own nails is irrelevant if you stick with false nails. However, if you plan to chop and change, it will take two or three months to get your nails back to their original condition, and if water gets trapped underneath a false nail, it can lead to a fungal infection, which is very difficult to clear.

the body

CHAPTER FIVE

When people judge how old you are, what do you think they look at first? Obviously your face is the main point of reference. Skin's pretty important, there's no denying that, but, as they say, beauty is only skin deep, and once someone is close enough to count your wrinkles, it's too late.

Before they get that far, however, your body will give them clues. Even from a distance your posture, walk, gestures, clothes, weight and energy send out clues for everyone to read. And you want to give out all the right messages long before anyone gets up close and personal.

In this chapter, we take a look at everything that's going on under the skin – your bones and muscles and how they contribute to the way you look. I'll be giving you tips and techniques on how to maintain a toned, youthful physique well into your 60s and beyond. With a balanced approach, you can actually reverse many of the effects of ageing on your body, so let's take a close look at the inside – your foundation.

YOUR BONES

When was the last time anyone told you that you have beautiful bones? OK, so your skeleton doesn't usually attract compliments, but it provides the scaffolding on which everything else hangs, so it's vitally important to the way you move and look. The sad fact is that, as you get older, the strength of your bones and connective tissue starts to deteriorate. During childhood it takes the skeleton just two years to renew itself; in adults it takes 7–10 years. After the age of 35 we start to lose bone, so the sooner you start investing in your 'bone bank', the better. Get back to basics and look after your bones, and they'll look after you.

My top tips

···⟩ Regular weight-bearing exercise will help you maintain bone density. This is particularly important for women because hormonal changes cause the bones to thin as we get older.

···⟩ Stay a healthy weight or you'll put stress on your bones. Too light and you may not be getting the nutrients you need. Too heavy and you'll put a strain on the soft tissue between the joints, which can result in injury.

···⟩ Take cod-liver oil – it's good for your skin and it neutralizes enzymes that eventually damage your cartilage.

···⟩ Take a supplement containing glucosamine, preferably with chondroitin. Both of these ease the symptoms of osteoarthritis and will help your body recover more quickly after exercise.

DID YOU KNOW?
A horrifying 200,000 fractures every year are caused by osteoporosis (brittle bones), and almost all of these are preventable. » When you exercise, you increase the levels of oestrogen and testosterone in your body; these in turn aid calcium absorption, which helps maintain the strength of your bones.

YOUR MUSCLES

Don't worry, I'm not suggesting body-building here – although each to his, or her, own – but you have to learn to love your muscles. Here's why:

···⟩ Your muscles make up half your body weight.

···⟩ Their tone and condition play a crucial part in your fitness and strength, as well as in your appearance.

···⟩ Without regular balanced exercise, your muscles waste. Think how little time it takes for a broken limb to become spindly after it has been encased in plaster. Fortunately they start to rebuild their bulk and strength as soon as you begin to use them again.

···⟩ Even if you keep up the same level of activity, your muscles reduce with age. Each decade you lose about 3 kg of lean muscle, and you have to do extra work to maintain it. Sadly, your metabolic rate gradually drops as you get older – by almost 5 per cent a decade once you pass 30. This means that you'll put on weight more easily, even if you eat the same amount and keep your activity levels constant. To maintain your weight, you're going to need to exercise more and eat less – or at least eat smarter.

···⟩ Increasing your muscle mass or lean body weight helps to boost your metabolic rate, which helps to keep your weight under control, as well as improving muscle tone. The large muscles in your bottom, fronts and backs of your thighs, stomach and upper arms are the ones that need most attention. When they're slack, underused and out of condition, they attract fat, fluid and toxins. Fortunately, these are the easiest muscles to exercise – even brisk walking goes a long way to toning them up.

Exercise

Yes, you knew it was coming, didn't you? Exercise is absolutely crucial for keeping your body, mind and spirit young. If you're a fully paid-up couch potato, you may find this hard to believe, but regular exercise can, and should, be fun. If the idea of thrashing around a gym or pounding the pavements is just too awful, there are plenty of stealthy ways to get moving. In this section I'm going to give you lots of hints and tips to combat love handles, bingo wings and much more. But first, try the quiz on page 116 to see whether you can sort out fact from fiction when it comes to exercise.

DID YOU KNOW?
After a year of regular light weight training, you can turn back your body clock by 15 to 20 years in terms of bone density, muscle bulk and strength, metabolism, flexibility, blood pressure and some of your hormone levels. » Losing muscle mass and strength is the underlying cause of almost every outward sign of ageing. Therefore, when you rebuild muscle, you regain youthfulness, stamina, energy and vigour.

HOW MUCH DO YOU KNOW ABOUT EXERCISE?

Try this quiz to see if you really know as much about exercise as you think you do.

1. Before, during and after exercise, I should do slow, static stretches. **True/False**

2. Not exercising regularly can be a major factor in premature ageing, illness and death. **True/False**

3. It's dangerous to exercise if you are over the age of 40. **True/False**

4. I've started to exercise, but I've gained weight. The exercise I'm doing isn't working. **True/False**

5. I would have to exercise for at least 30 minutes, three times a week to experience any benefits. **True/False**

6. Exercise won't do anything for my appearance and stress levels. **True/False**

7. Women don't build up muscle through exercise because they don't have enough testosterone. **True/False**

8. If you want to lose weight, you should exercise in the afternoon. **True/False**

9. Exercise has to be hard work or it's not doing you any good. **True/False**

10. Working with weights builds muscle, but does nothing for your heart. **True/False**

Check your answers here:

1. False Before and during your workout, slow, static stretching can lead to injuries. Before your workout you should do five to ten minutes of gentle aerobic warm-up to get your muscles ready – walking will do very nicely. Slow, static stretching is recommended only after your workout.

2. True You need physical activity to stay healthy throughout your life, even though you might not realize it when you're young. Every system in your body is affected by exercise, or the lack of it.

3. False You're never too old to start increasing your activity, as long as you're sensible and take account of your condition. The benefits are almost certain to outweigh the risks, but you should check with your GP before starting a new regime.

4. False Putting on weight can actually be a good sign. You might have lessened your body fat while adding lean muscle, both of which are signs that you're heading in the right direction and creating a more youthful body. Scales aren't necessarily good indicators of your fitness level. Instead, concentrate on how energetic you feel and on measurements, since although muscle weighs more than fat, it's denser, so that even if you weigh the same or more, you'll be trimmer.

5. False Any exercise is better than none, and if you're just starting, or you're particularly busy, doing whatever you can will keep the benefits coming in. Even five minutes' brisk walking shows benefits by reducing cholesterol and blood pressure, increasing bone density, stimulating your brain, fighting the flab and generally making you look and feel better. So never use lack of time as an excuse to avoid working out.

6. False Exercise can actually help everyone to reduce stress, sleep better and feel more energized.

7. False Testosterone is a factor in muscle development, but muscle size increase is more to do with genetics. If you are someone with a body type that tends to bulk up, use small weights and increase the number of repetitions you do. Regular exercise will improve and balance your hormone levels, including testosterone, which is important if you want to remain youthful looking. To ensure you're toning and not building muscle, always do 15 reps or more per set.

8. True At about 3 p.m. some of your hormone levels peak, making this an optimal period for weight loss. The late afternoon is also a good time to achieve high performance, if that's what you're after. Flexibility, strength and endurance are at their highest mid-afternoon, and working out at this time should improve your sleep patterns.

9. False What do you think I am? Some kind of masochist? Strenuous exercise may improve aerobic capacity faster than light or moderate workouts, but light to moderate exercise is just as good, if not better, at reducing stress, lowering high blood pressure, and aiding weight control. Provided you cover the same distance, you'll use up the same calories, so if you hate running, you can still achieve good results with walking, and incorporating yoga, Pilates or light weights will sculpt your body far better than running ever could.

10. False Give your heart a treat by combining strength and aerobic training. Both work in different ways to keep the arteries clear and both improve blood pressure, stress levels and stamina, all of which are important for a healthy heart.

It's not what you do but how you do it

To maintain optimal fitness and knock years off your age, develop a balanced approach to fitness. I work on the principle of the three S's – stamina, strength and suppleness – to cover all bases.

···⋗ For **stamina**, work on your aerobic fitness, raising your heartbeat and breathing a little faster by walking, running, dancing, cycling, having sex or skipping etc.

···⋗ To improve your **strength**, you need to exert your muscles in a controlled way, lifting weights, using resistance machines or the weight of your own body.

···⋗ Working on **suppleness** is vital if you want a free range of comfortable youthful-looking movement. Yoga, Pilates, t'ai chi and chi gung classes are ideal for this.

DID YOU KNOW?
On average, every minute of walking extends your life by up to two minutes. That's about a two for one trade-off.
» Walking an extra 20 minutes each day will burn off 3 kg of body fat a year.
» To burn off just one chocolate bean you need to walk the full length of a football pitch.

Here are a few tips to add to your routine:

···⋗ Interval training – working out hard for a couple of minutes, then easing off a little and repeating this pattern throughout the session – burns more calories, and stimulates your hormone levels more than working at the same rate throughout.

···⋗ If you're aiming to lose weight, try not to let more than 48 hours pass without exercise, because you need to keep your metabolic rate high if you want to burn fat. Remember that you need to work out three to four times a week to improve your condition, and once to twice a week to maintain it.

···⋗ Exercising on an empty stomach burns more calories than working out after a meal. However, a cup of coffee before you exercise can speed up the rate at which you draw on your fat reserves for energy – useful for weight loss, but not so good for your skin.

···⋗ Weight-training, even at fairly a low level, encourages the formation of lean tissue, which burns fat effectively, even when you're at rest. Add to this the benefits for bone density, and the firming effect that even a light-weights workout can bring, and you'll never look back. Trust me, weight training changed my life.

What's the ideal?

Follow this simple equation called the Broca formula for a rough idea of your ideal weight: your height in centimetres – 100 = your ideal weight in kilos

Are you really too fat?

I personally find that it's more emotionally healthy not to focus on your weight, but instead to judge your size on what feels right to you, especially if you're following my tips for a balanced, nutritional, anti-ageing way of eating. If you're unsure whether you're over- or underweight, you could calculate your body mass index (BMI) to find out how much fat is present in your body, and see how you compare to the World Health Organization's guidelines on the matter.

Calculate your BMI by dividing your weight in kilos by your height in metres, squared.

Example:
If you weigh 65 kilos and are 1.6 metres tall:
$65 \div (1.6 \times 1.6) = 65 \div 2.56 =$ a BMI of 25.39

The chart below gives the World Health Organization's ideal BMI:

16–18	underweight
18–20	tendency to underweight
18.5–24.9	normal weight
25.0–29.9	overweight
30.0–34.9	obesity (level 1)
35.0–39.9	obesity (level 2)
More than 40	extreme obesity (level 3)

'I'm not interested in age. People who tell you their age are silly. You're as old as you feel.'
ELIZABETH ARDEN

Somatopause for thought

...⟩ Weight gain
...⟩ Energy decline
...⟩ Loss of muscle definition
...⟩ Increase in bad cholesterol
...⟩ Poor sleep
...⟩ Loss of skin tone
...⟩ Bad moods

Any of this sound familiar? They're all symptoms of the 'somatopause', a gradual decline in condition that typically begins in your 30s. It seems the culprit for all this is the decline of HGH, or human growth hormone. It's been widely reported that several well-known actors take HGH injections for its anti-ageing, rejuvenating properties. And HGH has been banned for athletes because of its ability to improve performance. But guess what? You can make your own. All you have to do is exercise regularly and your levels of HGH start to rise again.

Hormone heaven

Exercise increases and rebalances many of your hormone levels, especially those that tend to decrease as you age. Reverse that trend and you can effectively reverse ageing. The table opposite lists just some of the hormones you can boost through exercise.

So there you have it: exercise is the single biggest influence on how youthful you look and feel, and it can slow down and even reverse the ageing process. On the following pages, we'll have a look at the ways you can tone your muscles, taking each part of the body in turn and focusing on specific exercises that will give you a trim and youthful physique.

HOW EXERCISE AFFECTS YOUR HORMONES

Hormone	Effect	Increase after exercise
Growth hormone (HGH)	Helps in the repair and growth of bones, tendons, ligaments, cartilage and muscle. Helps use up body fat during exercise. Improves sleep, mood, concentration, skin hydration and texture.	Increases after both aerobic exercise and weight training. Reaches its peak after 30 minutes' exercise.
Endorphins	Reduce tension, anxiety and appetite.	Up to 500 per cent increase after 30 minutes' moderate aerobic exercise.
Testosterone	Vital for both sexes to maintain muscle tone and strength. Increases metabolic rate and feelings of self-confidence. Reduces body fat. Improves orgasms.	Increases in blood after 20 minutes' aerobic exercise and weight training, and reaches a peak after 30. Remains higher for 1–3 hours.
Oestrogen	Elevates mood. Increases fat breakdown during exercise, metabolism and libido. Reduced level at menopause.	Increased by exercise and stays higher for 1–4 hours afterwards.
Thyroxine	Raises metabolic rate of almost all cells in body. Makes you feel more energetic and helps weight control. Makes skin renewal faster.	Blood levels increase by about 30 per cent during exercise and stay high for several hours afterwards. With regular exercise, levels are higher at rest too.
Epinephrine	Increases efficiency of heart. Breaks down fat for use as fuel.	Increases with length and intensity of exercise.
Insulin	Controls glucose levels in the blood and sends nutrients to the cells. With age, and if you're overweight, cells become resistant to insulin, so more is produced, resulting in stress on the pancreas and fat being deposited round the abdomen. Daily exercise and weight loss can improve this.	Blood levels begin to decrease after 10 minutes into an aerobic exercise session and continue to decrease through about 70 minutes of exercise. Regular exercise also increases cells' sensitivity to insulin at rest.
Glucagon	Raises blood levels of glucose and encourages breakdown of fat as fuel.	Released after 30 minutes of exercise when blood glucose levels decrease.

Shoulders, arms and hands

Do you hate to show your upper arms? Few things are more ageing than flabby biceps. Or how about bingo wings? When your upper arms keep on moving long after you've stopped waving. This horror is all down to your tricep muscles, and ballet, martial arts, light weights, swimming and tennis will all help tone them up. Here are some spot toners to try at home or in the gym.

Shoulder sculpting

You know that lovely firm, curved muscle that runs over your shoulder and down the top of your arm? Well, here's how to work on it. Stand with feet shoulder width apart, knees slightly bent and bottom tucked in. Pull up nice and tall through your spine. Now slowly raise both arms out at your sides, palms facing down, until they're in line with your shoulders. Don't raise your shoulders. In fact, concentrate on keeping your shoulder blades down, as this will help to keep your shoulders back too. Hold for a moment, then slowly lower. Once you've got the idea, start to use light weights and gradually build up.

Push-ups

---> Stand facing a wall, about a pace away. Place your palms flat against the wall at shoulder height. Inhale as you slowly bend your arms, elbows pointing downwards, and exhale as you straighten them again. Keep your back straight throughout. Start with five repetitions and gradually build up to 15.

---> Kneel on all fours, hands directly underneath your shoulders and fingers facing forwards. Inhale as you slowly bend your elbows and lower your face towards the floor. Exhale and straighten your arms again. Don't lock your elbows and keep your back straight throughout. As you get stronger, gradually move your knees further back, raise your feet and cross your ankles. Start with five repetitions and gradually build up to 15.

DID YOU KNOW?
With over 500 nerve endings per square centimetre, your fingers, thumbs and palms contain a third of the body's 5 million sensory fibres. You can hold a lot of tension in your hands, so try massaging your palms firmly with the knuckles of the other hand, then stroke firmly along the sides of each finger from base to tip using the thumb and forefinger. Better still, get someone else to do it for you.

Tricep dips

Sit on the edge of a strong chair or bench, with your hands on either side of your bottom, fingertips facing forward. Straighten your arms to raise yourself up and slide your hips forwards so your butt clears the edge of the seat. Gently lower your hips towards the ground, then straighten your arms to raise yourself back up. You are aiming to lower your body until your upper and lower arms are at 90 degrees, but this is quite strenuous, so build up to it. Start with five repetitions and gradually build up to 15.

Seated shoulder press

Sit on a chair with your feet flat on the ground. Hold a hand-weight/drinks bottle in each hand and raise your arms to the side, elbows bent and in line with your shoulders. Lift your arms from your shoulders up towards the ceiling, but keep your elbows slightly bent. Return to the starting position. Start with five repetitions and gradually build up to 15. Repeat with arms out to the sides.

Wrist curls

To keep wrists strong and the muscles of your forearm toned, bend your arms so that your lower arms are parallel to the floor and your elbows are tucked in at your sides. Hold a small weight – a kilo is plenty – and lift from the wrist, keeping your forearms still, first with the backs of the hands uppermost, then the palms. Work up to 20 repetitions.

Finger stretches

Keep your fingers supple and strong by slipping a sturdy rubber band over them, and spreading the fingers apart against the resistance. Repeat 20 times.

Grips

Hold a tennis ball lightly in the palm of your hand and slowly squeeze it, holding for about five seconds. Release and repeat 10 times with each hand. As you get stronger, work up to squeezing for 10 seconds.

WEIGHTS FOR FREE
Take two individual empty plastic drinks bottles that you can easily hold in your hands. Fill them part way up with water or sand, screw the tops on tightly and you've got weights you can slowly increase as you improve your muscle tone

Breasts

The skin on the breasts, chest and neck is as delicate and thin as that on your face, but without the benefit of the oil glands that constantly protect facial skin. It's an area where neglect shows very rapidly, through discoloration, dehydration and wrinkles, and as it's an area that tends to draw the eye, it pays dividends when you start to take care of it.

Top tips for perky boobs

⇢ Start early. Don't be tempted to go bra-less. Even if your breasts are small, the weight of them will stretch your skin and supporting tissue over time.

⇢ Always wear a well-fitting bra – it's amazing how many women wear absolutely the wrong size. Get yourself fitted properly and, if you retain lots of water before your period, have two sets of bras so that you have the perfect fit throughout the month.

⇢ Hand-wash bras and throw out all those grey, frayed and manky items. There are so many lovely bras available now that there's no excuse for wearing anything but the best. You deserve it!

⇢ Before you start to exercise, buy the best sports bra you can afford. Don't throw away all the other benefits of exercise by damaging your boobs.

⇢ When you shower, always finish off with a blast of cold water on your boobs to improve circulation.

⇢ When you moisturize the skin on your breasts, use the opposite hand to stroke firmly upwards towards the shoulder so that you don't drag the delicate skin downwards.

⇢ Wear your boobs with pride. Posture makes all the difference to their appearance.

DID YOU KNOW?
Rounded shoulders can reduce the bust by one whole cup size; standing properly will make them look twice as pert.

Boob exercises

If your boobs have started the long journey south, there's not much you can do about it. But firming up the underlying chest muscles (the pectorals) is always a good idea. Here's how:

⋯⋗ **Palm presses** Press the palms of your hands together at chest height and hold for a slow count of five, release and repeat.

⋯⋗ **Wash the windows** Boring, yes, but it's good for upper arms, upper back and boobs. The larger and more vigorous the movements, the better.

⋯⋗ **Perfect pecs** A chi gung exercise that strengthens shoulders, arms and pecs is simplicity itself. Stand with feet shoulder width apart, knees soft, back straight, and raise your arms to shoulder level, keeping your elbows softly rounded and palms facing you, as if you were hugging a big tree. Keep your shoulders down and feel your pecs tighten. Hold it for as long as is comfortable, then a bit longer.

⋯⋗ **Boob toner** Lie comfortably on the floor, with knees bent and feet flat. Using light weights and starting with no more than half a kilo in each hand, stretch your arms out to the sides at just below shoulder level, then slowly bring your hands together, keeping your elbows softly rounded. Open arms again to the floor. Work up to 20 repetitions.

DID YOU KNOW?
Much of the tension we carry around with us is held in the shoulders which, as the working day progresses, get higher and higher, until they're almost up to our ears. This is not a good look, and the tightness it causes is reflected in our facial skin and expressions, and in discomfort in the back. Try wearing long dangly earrings; when your shoulders touch your earrings, it's a gentle reminder to relax.

Back and posture

Back pain, as well as being excruciatingly unpleasant, makes you feel and look about a hundred because it restricts your movement so much. Around 40 per cent of adults suffer back pain in any given year, and once again our increasingly sedentary lifestyles are to blame.

Good posture is as important as eating, sleeping, exercise and not smoking. Bad posture is ageing – old people look hunched, as if they're having problems with their joints. Walking with round shoulders, made worse if you put your hands in your pockets and slouch, will immediately age you by 10 years.

When you get older the trunk of your body gets shorter because the discs between the spinal vertebrae become thinner through wear and tear, but arms and legs don't change. Older people often look out of proportion. By slouching you can give the impression that this is happening to you, which can put years on you. Correct posture, on the other hand, can add 2 inches to your height and make you look at least 2 kg lighter.

I can't say anything good about bad posture. It can lead to a pot belly, double chin, varicose veins, a hunched back, headaches, jaw ache, back pain and heart strain. And what's more, it can creep up on us when we least expect it. When we're stressed we release a hormone called cortisol, which causes our shoulders to rise towards our ears as if we're preparing for a fight. If you're not careful, good posture goes out the window, so you need to start imprinting good posture into your body so that you maintain a great shape no matter what you're doing.

> **DID YOU KNOW?**
> Your head weighs 5 kg on average, so by hanging the head you put strain on your back and spine, which will weaken the neck muscles, making you more and more round-shouldered (see page 126).

For perfect posture

⋯⇢ Stand with feet facing forwards and a few inches apart.

⋯⇢ Press down on the balls of your feet to distribute weight evenly.

⋯⇢ Tighten the muscles on the front of your thighs and in your bottom to stop your bum sagging.

⋯⇢ Draw buttock muscles together and you will feel your stomach tighten.

⋯⇢ Stretch your spine up and draw your shoulder blades together without lifting your shoulders or chin up and it will push your boobs out.

⋯⇢ Imagine you are a puppet with a long string, running through your body from your feet to the middle of your head, being pulled upwards.

⋯⇢ Read the posture tips on page 148 as well.

Exercising your back

One of the key elements of good posture is a strong, straight back. Lie on your front, forehead resting on the backs of your hands. Breathe out, tighten your stomach muscles and pelvic floor, and slowly raise one leg by about 10 cm, keeping it straight, but not tense. Feel as if you're extending it away, stretching and lengthening the leg as you do so. Lower, inhale and repeat 10 times with each leg.

⋯⇢ Still lying on your front, relax your legs and place your forehead gently on the floor. Raise your arms so you form a giant 'Y'. Breathe out and gently raise one arm by about 10 cm, again feeling a lengthening. Lower it and breathe out. Repeat 10 times with each arm.

⋯⇢ Once you can do both of these easily, try raising the opposite arm and leg, but alternate. Raise your left arm and right leg, then your right arm and left leg. Repeat 10 times for each pair.

> **DID YOU KNOW?**
> After the age of 40 we can shrink by 1 cm every 10 years. Over the course of a lifetime we can shrink as much as 7.5 cm, so standing tall helps, especially if it makes you 5 cm taller.

Pelvic floor

The band of muscle at the bottom of the pelvis supports the internal organs and is put under a lot of strain during your life, through childbirth, carrying heavy weights, squatting over public loos, etc. After your heart, it's probably the most important muscle you have, for posture, continence and keeping all your internal organs in place, and for both men and women, a healthy pelvic floor improves sexual enjoyment.

The best way to exercise your pelvic floor is to tighten and release it repeatedly. Imagine you're trying to stop yourself weeing, or are trying to hold a penny between your butt cheeks. You can do this anywhere – no one need ever know. Try it while you're going to the loo, during sex or even when you're on the phone.

Waist and stomach

These are prime places to put on weight, particularly when your metabolism slows down and your hormone levels start to drop. Fat build-up in this area is particularly ageing and really limits the types of clothes you can comfortably wear. There's only so far Lycra will stretch, and there's only so much you can camouflage with body-skimming tops. Face it, you're going to have to tone up. Love handles are just too unlovable.

Pilates and yoga are excellent ways of toning this area. Working on your core stability – the bit in the middle, in other words – not only gives you a trim, toned waist and stomach, but benefits the upper and lower parts of your body too. As well as joining a Pilates or yoga class, you can do these exercises at home.

DID YOU KNOW?
One of the best ways of toning up your pelvic floor is to have more sex. Not only will this release feel-good endorphins, it will add a youthful glow to your skin and burn up to a mammoth 300 calories per average session.

Stomach exercises

Your stomach consists of three muscle groups: top (upper abdominals), side (obliques) and lower abdominal muscles. It's important to work each muscle group when doing stomach exercises to ensure they're kept toned and honed.

Walk tall One of the best exercises for stomach muscles is simply to pull them in while you're going about your daily routine. Stand up tall, inhale then exhale, pulling in your stomach as tightly as you can. Focus on the muscles just below your navel and imagine pulling them inwards and upwards, towards your spine. Hold for five seconds, release and breathe in again. Repeat 10 times, and do it whenever you're waiting for a bus or for the kettle to boil. With regular practice, you'll start to see results within weeks.

Obliques Side stretches help to tone up the muscles at the sides of the waist, with knock-on effects for your stomach and back. Try standing against a wall to do these because it's very easy to twist if you do them free-standing. Stand up tall with your feet hip width apart. Breathe out as you lean over to one side, and breathe in as you come up again, then repeat on the other side. Start with 10 repetitions on each side and gradually work up to 20 repetitions.

Crunches Lie on your back with your feet flat on the floor and knees bent. Breathe out and pull in your stomach muscles, then gently raise your shoulders off the floor. Hold for a moment, then release. Keep the movement small. Repeat 10 times and gradually build up to 20 repetitions. From the same starting position, curl up, lifting your shoulders off the floor, taking care to support your neck. As soon as you feel your stomach muscles contracting, hold for 10 seconds, then release. This is quite hard going if you do it properly, so start with just 2 repetitions and gradually build up to 10.

Leg circles Lie on the floor with your knees bent and feet flat on the floor, hip width apart. Raise yourself up on your elbows and pull in your tummy muscles. Extend your right leg and make circles in the air with your foot. Repeat with your left leg. Start small and, as you get stronger, make bigger circles, building up to 30 seconds with each leg.

Bottom

Another sadly neglected part of the body. Firm, pert and taut is what you want in a bottom, because a neglected rear is a dead giveaway of your age. Work hard at these toning exercises and you can turn your pear into a peach.

Bottom exercises

Isometrics This is a fancy name for clenching your muscles to tone them up, and can be done almost anywhere. Try squeezing your butt muscles really tightly for the count of five, then release and do it again … and again. Do it when you're on the phone, waiting for a bus or waiting for the kettle to boil – anywhere, so long as you remember to do it. You'll see results in just a few weeks.

Bottom tucks Lie on the floor, knees bent and feet flat on the ground, hip width apart. Breathe in, exhale, pull in your stomach muscles and tense your buttocks at the same time, then slowly start to tilt your pelvis by flattening your back into the ground. Release and inhale, then repeat, lifting a little higher each time, until you start to peel your lower back off the floor. Go no higher than bra-strap level (men will just have to imagine this). Roll your back down slowly and enjoy the gentle massage your lower back gets at the same time.

Stair master Take the stairs two at a time for an intense toning treatment for thighs and butt. If you're unfit, start small and build up. It's a workout you can do almost anywhere.

Leg lifts Stand next to a firm support you can hold on to, with feet hip width apart. Raise your left leg out to the side, keeping your knee straight and your foot flexed, but keep the movement really small, just enough to feel the muscle in your butt tighten. Do 10 small raises like this, gradually building up to 20. Repeat, lifting the leg behind you, then repeat on the right.

Squat Stand upright with your feet pointing forwards and slightly wider than hip width apart. Reach your arms forward, bend your knees and sink as though you're about to sit in an invisible chair. Keep your weight over your feet to maintain balance and sink as far down as is comfortable. Hold for three seconds before returning to the starting position. Repeat 10 times.

Legs

Do you show your legs whenever the opportunity arises or keep them hidden away under trousers all year long? With a bit of TLC you can have pins to be proud of, and ones you'll enjoy showing off.

Exercise won't alter your bone structure, of course, so if you've got knobbly knees you're stuck with them. But regular exercise will tone and firm flabby calves and thighs, contour chunky ankles and firm your butt, as well as helping to counteract the effects of wearing high heels.

For toned thighs

Lunges Stand with your feet hip width apart, place your hands on your hips and pull your stomach in. Take a large step forward with your right foot, so that it's positioned directly underneath your right knee. Keep your left knee slightly flexed. Return to the starting position and repeat with the left leg. Start with five reps for each leg and build up to 10.

Pliés Stand with your hips slightly wider than shoulder width apart, feet turned out slightly, working from the hip. Tighten your butt and slowly bend your knees until you feel a slight pull in the front of your thighs. Slowly straighten up and pull up through your thighs. Repeat 10 times, gradually increasing to 20.

Curvaceous calves

Raises Stand with your feet parallel and hip width apart. Fix your eyes on a point at eye level and slowly rise up on your toes and back down again. Repeat 10 times, gradually increasing to 20. When you get really good, try doing this on one leg at a time.

High heel stretch Constantly wearing high heels puts a huge strain on your feet, ankles, legs and back, but not many women would give them up willingly. Give your calves a treat and place the phone book on the ground, stand up straight on it and let your heels hang over the edge so they touch the floor. Depending on where you live, this might be quite a challenge, but if the phone book isn't suitable, choose another book that stretches your Achilles tendon (the very tight, strong tendon that runs up from the back of your heel).

Feet

Poor old feet – neglected, covered up, squashed into confined spaces and often doused with strong-smelling sprays. On a good day, the most they can hope for is a shake of talc and maybe some anti-fungal cream. No wonder most of us dread exposing them in the gorgeous sandals that have been so popular in recent summers.

And yet feet are amazing things. Each one is made up of 26 bones arranged into four arches, two lengthways and two across. The 33 joints are moved by 19 muscles and held together by 107 ligaments. In the average lifetime your feet will carry you a staggering 65,000 miles. Don't you think they deserve better?

The good news is that a little regular care will make a big difference to your feet, both in terms of their appearance and the way they feel.

Foot exercises

···▷ **Rotations** From a seated position, raise one foot off the floor and slowly rotate your ankle, first clockwise, then anti-clockwise, 10 times in each direction. Repeat with your other foot.

···▷ **Curls** With your foot raised as before, curl your toes up tight, then stretch them out. Repeat 10 times with each foot.

These exercises can be done in front of the TV, so no excuses please.

DID YOU KNOW?
90 per cent of people have feet of different sizes – most only slightly, but it's worth getting your feet measured periodically just to keep an eye on things. Fit shoes to the larger foot and use padded inner soles to make the other one fit snugly. This will improve your posture and prevent back problems in later life.

YOUR SKIN

Now we get to the icing on the cake – your skin. But guess what? Most people neglect the skin on their bodies compared with that on their faces. How would you like to be exposed only for routine maintenance, dunked in hot water, scrubbed with soap, scraped with a razor, tugged at with strips of hot wax, sprayed with deodorants and, very occasionally, slapped with moisturizer before being squeezed into clothes virtually 24/7?

If your skin has lost its youthful bloom and is looking a bit blotchy and resentful, you can hardly blame it. Time to treat it with the respect it deserves. Don't forget it's your largest organ, and the skin on your body needs to be treated with care if you want it to look as youthful as the skin on your face.

Face creams have contained anti-ageing, antioxidant ingredients for years (see page 49), and now body creams are catching up fast.

Moisturize from within

It's all very well slapping on moisturizer, but as the skin acts as a waterproof layer on your body it needs to be moisturized on the inside as well as the outside. By eating foods rich in omega-3 and omega-6 fatty acids, beta carotene and vitamin E, you'll help to keep your skin healthy, fresh and soft, and you'll find all these nutrients and more in flax seeds, pumpkin seeds, sunflower seeds and oily fish.

The lower layer of your skin, the dermis, is where new skin cells are formed and it's nourished by the blood supply, so regular exercise all year round will improve the condition of your skin, helping to supply nourishment and remove waste products.

Skin problems

Neglected skin is unhappy skin, and the skin on your body may be trying to tell you something.

Goose-pimply skin on the upper arms and the backs of thighs is often a sign of irritated sebaceous glands, caused by a build-up of toxins and insufficient circulation.

Flabby areas, as well as crying out for attention to the underlying muscles, often suffer from fluid retention and fatty deposits, again due to sluggish circulation.

Dry, flaky skin can be caused by hormonal imbalance, sun damage, stress, poor diet and general neglect.

Spots and blocked pores are a sure sign that you need to address your skin from both sides – see Chapter 7 to help clean up your diet, and follow the tips overleaf.

Irregular pigmentation – age spots, to give them their proper and rather unpleasant name – are often a result of insufficient care when sunbathing. So if you're unhappy about the state of the skin on your body, don't ignore it, do something about it.

'If God had given a woman wrinkles, He might at least have put them on the soles of her feet.'

NINON DE LENCLOS, FRENCH COURTESAN

DID YOU KNOW?
For the best exfoliant money can't buy, mix three teaspoons of ordinary granulated sugar with your usual shower gel or bath oil and use it to scrub your skin. There's no need to rinse before getting into the bath as the sugar dissolves, taking your rough skin with it.

My top tips for bathtime bliss for mind, body and soul

Turn your bath or shower into an anti-ageing, rejuvenating treatment that will set you up for the night or day:

⋯▹ Exfoliate before you get into your bath using a cactus bristle brush, coarse sponge or an exfoliating product. Start with the soles of your feet to stimulate all those nerve endings and work up over the legs and trunk in long sweeping movements towards your feet, in the direction of your lymph. Next move onto your arms, again towards your feet. If you've used a body scrub with gritty bits in it, you might want to shower it off before you bathe.

⋯▹ Adding essential oils to your bath is a fantastic way to nourish your skin while unwinding after a busy day. If you do add essential oils to your bath, though, put them in at the last minute because they get broken down by heat. A few drops of sweet almond oil or wheatgerm oil added to your bathwater will coat your skin with the finest imaginable layer of oil that's high in nourishing vitamins A and E and quickly absorbed by the skin.

⋯▹ Don't wallow in a really hot bath: it ages your skin because excessive heat damages the cells that maintain firmness and tone. For the optimal bathing experience, soak for around 20 minutes. Any longer will dry out your skin. When you've finished, shower with tepid water to firm the skin.

⋯▹ Add a handful of powdered milk to your bath, swish it around and make like Cleopatra. Your skin will be softened and smoothed by the lactic acid in the milk, which gently exfoliates dead skin cells.

⋯▹ The steam from your bath opens up your facial pores, so take the time to cleanse your skin before you bathe and apply a moisturizing mask to your face and neck afterwards. A Henna wax or other hair treatment will also penetrate better in a humid atmosphere.

⋯▹ For a relaxing night-time bath, add 500 g of Epsom salts and 250 g of sea salt to your bath. Again, rinse thoroughly when you've finished soaking. Even better are Dead Sea salts, which are now incorporated in a number of good-quality bath products. They contain some 28 natural minerals which, when added to your bath, have a terrific detoxing effect, not just on your skin but on your internal system and stress levels.

⋯▹ Pat the skin dry and apply moisturizer while still slightly damp to lock the moisture in. Almond oil is light and quickly absorbed, but any good-quality body milk or cream will leave your skin silky and glowing. Use firm strokes when you apply it, working towards the heart, as you did with the bodybrushing.

Professional treatments

We've looked at various exercises and treatments that you can do to give yourself a youthful body. Sometimes, though, it's more fun, and definitely more indulgent, to let the professionals take over. Treating yourself and your body makes you feel and look great.

For massage, there are so many to choose from – relaxing, invigorating, with sea salts or exotic fruits, hot stones or cold mud – that I would need another book just to go through them all. Go along to your local beauty salon or health spa to see what they have to offer. A full body massage stimulates the circulation from top to toe, which perks you up, banishes depression and makes you feel good.

Hypoxitherapy

This eliminates cellulite and burns fat by cycling and exercising under low atmospheric pressure for 30 minutes, while simultaneously increasing the blood supply and improving the circulation to cellulite- and fat-prone areas such as the hips, thighs and buttocks. A full course of hypoxitherapy treatments is held over four, six and eight weeks and requires you to attend three treatments a week. The best results are achieved when treatments are taken on alternate days during the week. It's not cheap, though, at around £450 for the recommended 12 sessions.

Body wrap

This is where you do your impersonation of Tutankhamun and it's a very effective detox for the skin, plus you can lose 25–30 cm from one treatment. You're wrapped in marine clay-soaked bandages, which are applied to each part of the body. Fat is compressed and some impurities are purged through the pores, while the remainder is flushed internally via the lymphatic system. The treatment results in smoother elastic fibres, tighter skin, firmer fatty tissues and reduced bloating from fluid retention, giving a more contoured, sculpted appearance and softer skin. Treatments from around £45 per session.

Colonic irrigation (or colonic hydrotherapy)

Not for the faint-hearted, this really cleans and detoxes your system from the inside out. Fifty litres of water are flushed gently through the colon to remove dead tissue, impacted faeces and mucus. Not for people with high blood pressure, haemorrhoids, Crohn's disease or pregnant women. Costs around £60 per treatment.

DID YOU KNOW?
5,600 people a month in the UK have colonic irrigation.

Cosmetic treatments and surgery

Whether you opt for a peel or a needle, cosmetic treatments and surgery can radically alter your skin. I make no apologies for starting this section with a warning. If you choose to take this route, go to a qualified practitioner, because if done badly, these treatments can cause serious, and sometimes permanent, damage.

Do your research. Don't just talk to one salon or clinic: go to at least three before choosing. Ask for referrals, before and after photographs, case studies and details of the treatment, and if you don't understand what's involved, ask again. Find out what you can expect and ask if there are any side-effects.

If you're not happy with the results, complain to the practitioner or the clinic. If you aren't happy with their response, contact the GMC (see page 280) if the procedure was carried out by a doctor, or the Nursing and Midwifery Council (see page 280) if it was performed by a nurse. If the treatment has caused you personal injury, you could seek advice from the charity Action for Victims of Medical Accidents (see page 280), or from a specialist solicitor.

It's important to make sure you are as healthy as possible before the operation because your recovery time will be affected if you aren't in good shape. Achieve a healthy weight beforehand, give up smoking and make sure you eat a balanced diet and take plenty of exercise.

Liposuction

A narrow tube is inserted through a small incision and used to vacuum the fat layer that lies beneath the skin. The tube is pushed then pulled through the fat, breaking up the fat cells and suctioning them out through a vacuum pump or large syringe. Areas suitable for liposuction include the abdomen, thighs, hips, buttocks, male chest and smaller areas such as the chin and knees. It's designed to change the shape of your body. Don't expect to have all your excess fat removed at once. Too much (a litre or more) can be dangerous. The procedure needs a general anaesthetic and can be painful during recovery. You will need an experienced surgeon. Fat taken from the body can also be used elsewhere to plump things up a bit. Costs from £2,900–£5,400.

Abdominoplasty (tummy tuck)

This will get rid of excess fat around the waist and remove excess skin to leave a flatter, lower body profile and younger-looking abdomen. If you intend to lose a lot of weight or plan to have future pregnancies, postpone the surgery until afterwards, as vertical muscles in the abdomen that are tightened during surgery can separate again during pregnancy. Costs around £5,600.

Apronectomy (mini-tummy tuck)
This procedure is similar to a full abdominoplasty, except that the navel doesn't need repositioning. It normally produces excellent results and the effects are generally long lasting, provided you follow a balanced diet and exercise regularly. Costs around £4,400.

Breast surgery

You can have a breast enlargement, reduction or lift. The procedure takes place under general anaesthetic and is done by a qualified plastic surgeon.

Enlargement The implants used are a silicon rubber shell filled with medical-grade silicon gel or a salt-water solution known as saline. Costs from £3,500–£4,200.

Reduction The aim of this surgery is to have smaller, shapelier breasts in proportion to the rest of the body. Excess breast tissue, fat and skin are removed and the nipples and remaining underlying tissues are then moved to a new, higher location. From £4,100–£5,200.

Uplift This procedure is used to surgically raise and reshape droopy or saggy breasts to improve their appearance, sometimes using implants. Costs from £4,200–£5,300.

Obagi Blue Peel (TCA)

I talked about peels in Chapter 2, but they can also be applied to other parts of the body. This chemical peeling treatment can be used on the face as well as other parts of the anatomy, such as the neck, hands, back, arms, chest and legs. The Obagi Blue Peel removes thin surface layers of aged and damaged skin. The underlying skin is then stimulated to form a revived and rejuvenated surface with improved skin clarity and texture, producing a healthier and more youthful appearance. Costs from £1,000.

DID YOU KNOW?
40 per cent of women would consider cosmetic surgery. The most popular procedures are stomach tucks and liposuction.

Our wonderful, complex, marvellous bodies are something to celebrate, but sometimes we treat them as if they were a pair of old jogging bottoms – unloved and uncared for. It makes such a big difference if we treat our bodies with a little care. Not only do we feel good physically, but that sense of wellbeing shines through. Mark Twain said, 'The finest clothing made is a person's own skin,' and I have to agree with him. So treat your body as if it were a couture gown from a top designer: care for it, protect it and above all love it.

attitude

CHAPTER SIX

Age is a funny thing. When we were young, extra years were something to be coveted. Think of the how precise children are when asked their age: 'I'm six and three-quarters' or 'I'll be a teenager next June'. Then almost overnight our attitude to age changes and we're far less keen to acquire extra years. Much of this book has been about the physical. But if you really want to look 10 years younger on the outside, you need to start thinking young on the inside too.

Too many of us start to act old before our time, and when that happens it becomes a self-fulfilling prophecy. We take the lift rather than bounce upstairs, and before long we couldn't bounce up the stairs if we tried. Elasticated waists seem like a good idea, and we find ourselves ignoring fashion and what suits us in favour of the comfortable, and usually less flattering, option.

But the good news is that we're living longer than any previous generation and have more beauty products, healthy foods and life opportunities open to us than ever before, all of which help keep us looking and feeling fantastic. Twenty years ago, middle age was defined as early 40s. Now most people would estimate it as 50s. You're as young as you feel, so stop acting old.

So far, scientists haven't found a gene for ageing. Obviously, our genes have a huge impact on our bodies and our lives. But how we live with those genes is up to us. About 50 per cent of our personality is fixed by our genes, and 10 per cent is influenced by life events. That leaves around 40 per cent of our personality to be filled, and it's entirely up to the individual how they choose to do that.

Attitude has as much of an effect on our bodies as our genes, and what we feel inside will show on the outside. I'm not trying to create a race of Stepford wives, rather happy, confident individuals. This book is about empowering you and giving you inspiration.

'If a woman knows she's pretty, it's not because some other woman told her so.'

ANONYMOUS

IT'S ALL IN THE MIND

The mind is probably the most powerful part of your body. I always say, 'If you believe it, you can achieve it.' A positive attitude can do more for your appearance and approach to life than anything else. Just think of some of the positive people you know. It's as if they're painted in brilliant Technicolor. They *adore* this, *love* doing that, can't *stand* it when such and such happens. In other words, they're full of life and appreciate every aspect of it, the downs as well as the ups.

Positive people are wonderful to be around. They radiate an energy we find attractive. Like moths around a flame, we're drawn to that energy and want to be part of it. More importantly, a positive approach to life raises your energy levels, and if you're feeling bright and bubbly, you look and feel younger.

A negative approach to life is bad for your health. That's official. Hundreds of studies show that compared to pessimists, optimists are higher achievers and healthier individuals. Happy people have higher levels of antibodies and can fight off infection more easily. What's more, optimists live an estimated seven and a half years longer than pessimists.

So accentuate the positive:

⋯⋗ Remember the times when you were feeling happy and confident.
⋯⋗ Fake a smile. Studies found that people who pretended to frown began to feel angry, while the fake smilers started to feel happy.
⋯⋗ Use your body to show confidence – head up, shoulders back.
⋯⋗ Enjoy 7 p.m. – according to a survey by Cadbury, it's the happiest time of the day for most people because we're at home with our family and have the rest of the evening ahead of us.
⋯⋗ Try not to use words like 'can't', 'shan't', 'wouldn't' or 'shouldn't'. Negative words can wreak havoc on positive thinking.
⋯⋗ Focus on the positive things that have happened to you, not the negative
⋯⋗ Have photos around that remind you of some of your happiest moments.

DID YOU KNOW?
Laughing can burn off the same amount of calories as climbing two flights of stairs.

A big, friendly smile is 90 per cent of what people see when they meet you – not how old you are, not what you're wearing, not what kind of hairstyle you've got. So go dazzle them.

Smiling and laughing exercise facial muscles and keep them toned. But even the sunniest personalities can wake up feeling a bit down. If that happens to you, don't be tempted to indulge the mood. Put on a gorgeous outfit so you can face the world looking fabulous. Whoever you bump into, whatever the day throws at you, if you look well turned out and styled, you can deal with it because you know you'll look good to everyone else. This is all about being kind to yourself. Hold on to those feel-good emotions and use them to switch off the negative ones.

That's not surprising when we're bombarded with media images of young, slim, beautiful people. No wonder women worry that they're too old, too fat, too imperfect. But you are *so* much more than your size, shape and weight. Don't worry about what others think of you; if you feel good about yourself, that positive, youthful glow will shine through. Beauty is all about confidence, not whether you're a size eight or not. It's true what they say, beauty does come from within.

So stop being hard on yourself. Take control of how you look and you'll feel more confident. Focus on yourself and how unique you truly are. Love your best bits, listen to your body, treat it with respect and you can look years younger.

DID YOU KNOW?
Within 10 seconds of meeting you, a person will have formed up to 11 opinions about you. » Eight out of ten women are unhappy with the way they look.

Easy ways to improve posture

Slimness is associated with youth. You can look 3 kg leaner instantly just by standing up straight. Rounded shoulders and a torso like a sack of potatoes will make anyone, no matter how lovely, look older, heavier and droopier. So keep checking your posture – it's good for your back and it's good for your looks. Walk like a leaner, slender, younger person and you'll start to look like one too.

···› Think of centring your body over the balls of your feet.
···› Try walking along a narrow kerb – it will stop you walking with your feet too far apart.
···› When you sit your shoulders should be balanced over your hips – don't slump.
···› When lifting heavy objects always bend your knees.
···› Practise contracting your pelvic floor muscles – squeeze as if you want to stop yourself having a pee and consciously tighten your abdominal muscles. Within three weeks your posture will be noticeably better.
···› Imagine there's a piece of string joined to the top of your head and someone is gently pulling you up with it. You'll literally stand taller.

THE INNER CHILD

Growing older does have its advantages, of course. You get to stay out late, you're mistress of your own destiny, you can eat cornflakes when you want and you can paint your nails any colour you damn well please. But don't forget the pleasures of childhood as well. Remember how carefree we all were as children? No responsibilities – that was for the grown-ups. Being young at heart is all about attitude and nothing to do with age.

Memories from childhood can be a powerful tool in keeping both your attitude and outlook youthful. Try to recreate those memories. For me, the sound of the sea takes me back to childhood holidays. For others, it can be the smell of a Sunday roast or the feel of crisp, white cotton sheets that takes them back to those golden days when they were young.

If you have children yourself, don't use them as an excuse for getting old: help them to keep you young. Come down to their level and remember what fun being young is. I popped out to the shops with my friends' four-year-old daughter recently, and what should have taken 10 minutes stretched to half an hour because we didn't step on the cracks in the pavement in case 'the bears at the corner of the street' got us. It was wonderful, giggly fun that left me feeling full of life. So don't sit on the sidelines watching children play – join in. Take a leaf out of their book and learn to play like a child.

DID YOU KNOW?
Children smile about 400 times a day.
Adults only smile an average of 15 times.

Reclaim your inner child

⋯⋗ Have a pillow fight.
⋯⋗ Lie on your back, look up at the sky and make pictures in the clouds.
⋯⋗ Jump in puddles.
⋯⋗ Eat ice cream straight from the tub.
⋯⋗ Buy a boy/girl band CD and dance your socks off.
⋯⋗ Discover your inner daredevil and do something wild.
⋯⋗ Go to a quiet spot and scream.
⋯⋗ Stay curious; children are always asking why.
⋯⋗ Take off your clothes and dance around the house – though you might want to draw the curtains first!

Remember what it was like getting ready as a teenager? Your music was on loudly in the bedroom, you danced around as you got dressed and you waltzed out of the house on a high, feeling and looking great. You don't have to be a teenager to still do that. In a poll by the charity MIND, Robbie Williams' 'Let Me Entertain You' came out top as the best feel-good song, followed by 'Walking On Sunshine' by Katrina & The Waves.

'The great thing about getting older is that you don't lose all of the other ages you have been.'

MADELEINE L'ENGLE, WRITER

RELAXING

We are human beings, not human 'doings'. When doing gets too much, you must learn to stop, relax and just start being you.

Having objectives in life is not a bad thing. But when you're constantly striving towards goals, you run the risk of finding dissatisfaction instead. If you're using up all your energy to make life better in the future, you tend to miss out on enjoying what life has to offer *now*. Living for the moment, appreciating what's around you rather than constantly planning for something a few months ahead will help boost your happiness and frame of mind. 'Stop and smell the roses' is a fabulous mantra. And if you're happy and relaxed, guess what? You look younger.

A little bit of stress doesn't do any harm; in fact, it's a necessary and good part of life. But constant stress keeps our bodies in a high state of alert, which means tense muscles, high blood pressure and digestive problems. It's hard to look glowing, gorgeous and ten years younger with all that going on.

If you're not stressed now, a time will come when you probably will get uptight. And when you get uptight, you get tense and hunched and look anything but youthful. At that point, it's difficult to calmly switch off the stress and think relaxing thoughts. So write down ten things that make you happy and relaxed. On my list, I'd include phoning a good friend for a chat; taking a long, luxurious bubble bath; enjoying a glass of fabulous champagne; planning a weekend in the country (I love the anticipation as much as the weekend itself) and walking by water – whether it's the sea, a river or a lake it doesn't matter. I'm a water sign and water makes me feel great.

DID YOU KNOW?
According to the Health & Safety Executive, 6.5 million paid sick days were taken in 2003 because of stress.

⋯⇢ When life gets on top of you, take out your list and pick one thing from it to make you feel better and more relaxed.

⋯⇢ Try to hold back that stress and tension by putting pleasure into your everyday life. Even the most mundane things can bring enjoyment. Serve yourself a cup of tea in a beautiful bone china teacup and saucer and daydream while you drink it. Light some candles when you have your evening meal. Buy yourself some fresh flowers. Greet people with a smile.

⋯⇢ At the end of the day, make a point of shrugging off any tension. Breathe in and tighten your shoulders, pulling them up to your ears. Then exhale gently while relaxing your shoulders. Do this three times and feel the knots and anxiety slip away.

⋯⇢ If you feel like some real indulgence, treat yourself to a massage. A full body massage not only boosts the circulation, getting blood flowing freely round the body from head to toe, it also releases those old friends endorphins, which reduce depression, give us a feeling of well-being and banish tensions.

'One cannot think well, love well, sleep well, if one has not dined well.'

VIRGINIA WOOLF

Tips to reduce stress

···⟩ Say 'yes' to the things you like, 'no' to the things you don't.

···⟩ Repeat after me, 'I am not indispensable'. Cut down your commitments and say if you don't have time for something.

···⟩ Learn to delegate. Yes, you probably could do things more quickly by yourself, but you'll only get more frazzled.

···⟩ Sit cross-legged with your back straight. Breathe in through your nose until your tummy swells,then tighten it to push the air out. Do this for 20 breaths and feel your vitality and energy grow.

···⟩ Take up yoga – it energizes and relaxes you as well as helping you look younger thanks to the extra blood and oxygen that flood your cells, giving you toned, fresh-looking skin.

···⟩ Watch a weepy film and have a good cry. Crying is a way of flooding our bodies with oxygen, which in turn triggers the release of feel-good transmitters to the brain.

···⟩ Remember good posture: it prevents tension building in your body. So head up, chin level, shoulders down, eyes focused.

···⟩ Live for today and try not to worry about what has been and what might happen. Use that precious energy for here and now.

···⟩ Pace yourself – does everything have to be done at top speed?

···⟩ Turn off your mobile from time to time. Be unavailable and use that precious time for yourself. If you're really brave, try doing without technology – phone, fax, computer, mobile – for a whole day.

···⟩ Learn a bit from wild animals and stop doing anything for your kids that they can actually do for themselves. You're meant to be teaching them, not serving them.

DID YOU KNOW?
Good Housekeeping magazine found that 30 per cent of women say they can't live without their mobile phone for more than a day.

SLEEP

The ultimate form of relaxation. I'm a massive sleeper – eight hours a night. And if I don't get those eight hours, I'll catch up with a nap at the weekend. The average person needs seven hours, plus or minus an hour depending on the individual. Sleep is vital to your well-being, but not sleeping can be a common problem: over one in three people will suffer from insomnia at some time in their lives.

We've already looked at some ways of winding down and getting to sleep in the last chapter. What you eat and drink can help or hinder a good night's sleep.

Get into a routine before you go to bed. Sylvia Plath had a point when she said, 'There must be quite a few things that a hot bath won't cure, but I don't know many of them.' A warm bath is more than just getting yourself clean. Use the time to relax, wind down, connect with your inner self and feel good. Add some relaxing music, read a book, do some gentle stretching, whatever suits you, and you'll soon be ready for bed. Even that old standby a glass of milk helps, thanks to the sleep-promoting tryptophan that it contains. By winding down like this after a busy day you're stimulating the release of endorphins, which help you relax.

Don't fight a yawn – it's nature's way of relaxing your body. If you feel a yawn on its way, let it out. But if you're somewhere that yawning isn't appropriate, try a long, deep sigh instead – it has the same effect.

If you're in bed and finding it difficult to get to sleep, try this easy relaxation exercise:
- Lie on your back and focus on your body.
- Starting with your feet, work your way up your body, tensing each main set of muscles (feet, calves, thighs, bottom and so on), then relaxing them.
- When you've done your face (jaw, eyes, forehead), press your head firmly back into your pillow and relax.

···▷ Now concentrate on your breathing – try making the out breath slightly longer than the in breath.

···▷ Leave a small pause between breathing in and out.

···▷ The concentration will clear your mind and the breathing will relax your body.

Exercising in the late afternoon or early evening will help you feel tired at bedtime. Run a warm (not too hot) bath, with a few drops of essential oil, such as lavender, to help relax the mind and muscles. Finally, a drop or two of lavender or chamomile oil on your pillow will help you enjoy a good night's quality sleep. Make sure your bedroom is dark and quiet and that your bed is comfortable and neither too hot nor too cold.

SEX

Enjoy romance. Some of our happiest moments are during sex with a loving partner. It may not always be hot and raunchy, but that doesn't matter. Remember it's also an act of love between a couple, the glue that keeps a relationship together and creates feelings of love, trust, approval and warmth. And, just as importantly, sex makes us feel young.

Regular sex also helps fight sickness. Scientists in the USA tested people's levels of immunoglobulin A, which is the first line of defence against flu and colds. Those who had sex once or twice a week had 30 per cent higher levels in their body than those who had less frequent sex.

Orgasms don't just put a spring in your step, they can relieve tension, act as a natural tranquillizer and produce phenetylamine, which helps to reduce your appetite.

So sex is a good thing. Great for feeling fit, healthy and youthful. But let's face it, we don't all walk around feeling like a sex goddess every day. Work, family and stress can all be passion killers. Sex appeal is about confidence and spirit. *Think* about sex – the brain is your largest, most powerful erogenous zone.

In order to be sexy, you need to *act* sexy. The more you like your body, the more sexy you'll feel, as feelings follow behaviour. So in order to feel sexy:

- Smell nice. If you smell sexy, you'll feel in the mood. Perfumiers say that floral notes make you feel feminine and pampered.
- Always wear gorgeous underwear and dig out those high heels or pretty shoes – it's hard to feel sensuous in trainers.
- Dance seductively by rolling your pelvis like a belly dancer.
- Create the mood – light a few candles and burn some essential oils.
- Give your partner a massage – use essential oils such as jojoba, jasmine and bergamot for men, or neroli and geranium for women.
- Remember all the things you find attractive about your partner.
- Look after yourself so you're always ready for sex – keep your bikini line waxed and maintain lovely feet. There's nothing worse than being seduced by some drop-dead gorgeous man only to realize you're in no state to be seen undressed.

Enhancing libido

Most of us, at some time in our lives, go through a period of low libido.
This is absolutely normal and doesn't mean your relationship is on
the decline, nor is it likely to go on for very long. Relax, sex should be
something that happens when you want it to, not because you feel you
should be doing it. But if you want to reawaken that loving feeling,
try some of these suggestions:

···⟩ Have sex somewhere other than bed. Remember when you didn't
always have access to a bed so anywhere would do? Try making love
in an unusual place so that you feel like young lovers again.
···⟩ Enjoy a long, steamy shower or warm bath together.
···⟩ Making love doesn't need to be full-blown sex – treat each other to
cuddling and touching, then just see what happens next.
···⟩ Have sex when your mind is clear and you have time to really enjoy it.
Making love while thinking about work/the children/cleaning the
house is never going to be a great turn-on.
···⟩ Don't let sex become too routine. Change the times when you have
sex – if you usually do it at night, try starting the day with some fabulous
frolicking instead.
···⟩ Make love even when you don't really feel like it – before you know
it, you will be in the mood.

ENERGY

What is this energy that we all talk about? Without energy, it's hard to function properly, let alone look youthful and radiant. True, lack of energy can often be caused when there's something not quite right with your body, but experts have now come round to thinking that low energy levels can come from what's going on in your mind, not just what's happening to your body.

Your mood and how you behave can affect you physically. If you feel drained, low and tired, guess what? You'll look it too. Scientists have discovered that the red blood cells of people who are depressed or stressed carry less oxygen. The less oxygen in your blood, the less energy you have, so you need to manage your oxygen levels carefully.

- Don't waste your energy. Think of it as money – you wouldn't waste your cash on something you didn't need or want. Prioritize what you want and forget the rest.
- Using energy wisely, such as exercising, will boost your mood for at least two hours afterwards and increase your energy levels.
- Never underestimate the energy-increasing power of a quick nap – I swear by them.
- Avoid energy drainers such as caffeine, which create rollercoaster highs and lows.
- Tackle the things in your life that are draining your energy. If the house is really getting you down, get a cleaner. Or maybe a friendship is becoming so high maintenance that it's draining you – learn to say no.

DID YOU KNOW?
If you stand up when you're on the phone, not only will you feel and sound more confident, you'll actually burn about 120 calories an hour – nearly 50 more than if you remain seated.

KEEPING YOUTHFUL

I've said it not once, but several times: if you believe in something, you'll achieve it. The power of the mind is awesome. Looking 10 years younger comes from attitude as much as diet, exercise and make-up. Being youthful is a state of mind.

Don't get stuck in a rut. Always be prepared to change or experiment. Just because something worked for you when you were 21 – whether it's a certain hairstyle or the way you wore your eye make-up – doesn't mean it still looks good 10 or 20 years on. In fact, it probably makes you look older than you are.

Exercise is a great way to stay looking young. You don't have to run marathons or work out in the gym seven days a week – a brisk five-minute walk can stimulate your brain, thanks to an increase of blood and oxygen, and perk you up as the body's natural mood-boosting chemicals get into the bloodstream. It will also help lower your cholesterol and blood pressure, increase your bone density and tone your body. As the oxygen races round the body, more collagen is produced, which gives your skin a better texture and youthful glow. What's more, walking's free and you can do it any time. Stop finding excuses *not* to do something and become a make-it-happen person.

···> Stay socially active; people with strong social networks are livelier, healthier and have more self-esteem.
···> Keep your mind active.
···> Go dancing – at home or in a class. Music has a wonderful energy that can lift your spirits and change your mood.
···> Get out into the countryside. People who live in the country live on average eight years longer than town and city dwellers. I live in London, but love weekends in the country.
···> At least once a week set aside time to do something you love – have a night out with friends, watch a film, go for a massage or pursue a hobby. It doesn't matter what it is as long as it makes you happy.

··❖ Being older doesn't mean you can't try new fashions. Don't be afraid
to try on things you've never worn before – experiment and have fun.

··❖ Try to spend at least 10 minutes outside. Natural light increases our
serotonin levels.

··❖ Surround yourself with yellow – experts say it makes us feel playful
and creative – and orange, which is supposed to make us feel confident,
resourceful, lusty and adventurous.

As Mae West said, 'Too much of a good thing is wonderful.' While I've
talked about sensible eating, a good diet and so on, I'm not suggesting
that from now on you live like a nun. Be young at heart and have a good
time. As a friend once said to me, 'My body is a temple, but it's also an
amusement park.' As long as you get the balance right – and don't spend
too long on the rollercoaster – you can have fun and enjoy life.

At least once a day, do something purely for yourself and nobody
else. Don't feel guilty about wanting to look and feel great: you're worth
it. Take control of yourself and your life. Think about your strengths and
build on them; they are the route to feeling happy, secure and confident.
Feel ugly and old and that is what the world will see. Feel vibrant and
glowing and everyone will see it.

Much of someone's perceived age depends on their behaviour.
Walk like a 20-year-old, smile like a child, have the audacious confidence
of a teenager, bluff and blag it, be silly, be flirtatious, just enjoy being.
If you start feeling 10 years younger, you'll soon start to look it too.

Life isn't a dress rehearsal. This is it, so make it good, great and
enjoyable. I think of life as an adventure and I'm constantly exploring,
discovering and looking. Be open to new things and new ways.
Looking 10 years younger is more than skin deep – it's an attitude.

nutrition

CHAPTER SEVEN

A good friend of mine once put diesel in her beloved new sports car instead of petrol. It was never the same again. Even after it had been fully drained and cleaned out, its performance was always sluggish and it drove like a car four times its age.

Luckily, our bodies are slightly more forgiving – we can make the odd mistake and have the occasional indulgence and still perform pretty well. But consistently filling up on the wrong foods will eventually take its toll. If you really want to look 10 years younger, diet is key. And the results can be pretty dramatic. Research shows that some simple dietary changes can transform your complexion in just one week.

First, let me make one thing clear: I am absolutely not talking about dieting. Dieting does not work. Most people who diet end up back at their starting weight or, worse, they gain a few pounds. Even if your diet is 'successful' and you lose a lot of weight, you'll end up with one of the most ageing things of all – saggy skin.

What I'm talking about here is healthy eating, day in, day out – as much a part of your lifestyle as cleaning your teeth or taking a bath. And stop panicking: I'm not talking about dull eating plans and a lifetime of self-denial, but dead easy ways to alter your eating habits and to have you looking and feeling younger. You will feel so good that you won't want to go back to your old ways.

I am passionate about healthy eating. As a qualified dietician, I've seen so many people literally transformed by a few basic changes of diet. They don't just look younger, they're healthier, they have more energy, they function better and they feel great. If you want fabulous, youthful skin, healthy shiny hair and strong, attractive nails, you must tackle them from the inside. Not only can the right diet help time stand still, but many fantastic foods actually reverse the signs of ageing. Nature can provide us with all the nutrients we need. Supplements are fine and I actually take a couple myself, but if you eat the right foods you'll get everything your body needs to look youthful, not to mention fantastic.

I'm not into being prescriptive; I'll share my favourite tips and secrets with you, but you don't have to follow them slavishly. Pick and mix the ones that work best for you. Grinding your way through plates of food that you don't like would be madness, and you won't stick to it — eating should be one of life's great pleasures. There are so many foods that can help boost the way you feel, improve your skin, kick-start your metabolism, increase your libido and knock back the years. Find the right ones for you and enjoy.

And please, if you do have the occasional 'bad' day, don't give up and go back to your old ways. You wouldn't stop sleeping just because of one bad night, so don't give up on healthy eating after one day of indulgence.

KEEP ON MOVING
Seven prunes a day will give you all the antioxidants your body needs.

MY TOP TEN TIPS FOR HEALTHY EATING

1. Water is wonderful!

I always start the day with a cup of warm water and a slice of lemon. It's a fabulous way to wake up the mind and body, and the lemon juice helps to increase the skin's natural elasticity. Warm lemon water will go straight through your body, helping to purge all those ageing toxins.

Then just keep it flowing all day. Water is, simply, your body's most fundamental beauty treatment. Most skin specialists now recommend drinking at least eight glasses (2 litres) of water a day. Without enough water you literally dry up – ever heard a prematurely old-looking woman described as an old prune? And don't wait until you feel thirsty before pouring yourself a glass, because as you age, your thirst mechanism fails to function as well as it should. I find that the more water I drink, the more thirsty I become, making it easy to keep on drinking.

The effects of drinking water will be really rewarding. Water literally hydrates the skin, eliminating fine lines, flushing out harmful toxins and reducing puffiness. Drinking water is something you can start doing right now – it's free and it's the easiest way to beat the clock. Within just a few hours of drinking plenty of water your skin will feel noticeably softer. Drink water regularly for a week and you'll see an improvement in the mirror. What are you waiting for?

2. Beware of fruit juices

Often packed with sugar, fruit juices can quickly pile on the pounds: a large glass of orange juice will set you back about 120 calories. Try eating your fruit juice instead – cut an orange into segments and eat it with your breakfast. It'll take you longer to consume, there won't be any hidden additives, it'll be absolutely fresh and unprocessed, and you'll get twice your recommended daily intake of vitamin C. Plus – and this is the best bit – that orange will have half the calories of the glass of juice.

3. Go brown

Your undies should be whiter than white, but not your food. If it's white, it's probably highly processed and stripped of all the goodness. So when you're reaching for some pasta, pitta, sugar, rice or bread, put the white stuff back on the shelf and choose brown; it will satisfy your hunger more.

4. Don't dump dairy

Dairy foods get a bad press, but they have a
vital role to play in a healthy diet and actively
help keep you feeling young. I eat natural
yoghurt almost every day of my life to ensure
my calcium levels are good. If you don't look
after your bones, you may not look older,
but you'll certainly feel it.

DID YOU KNOW?
You're better off drinking water at room-temperature or even warm: ice-cold water
chills your stomach, making it absorb nutrients less efficiently. » Between 50 and
60 per cent of your total body weight is water. 85 per cent of the brain is water and
75 per cent of the upper body's water is stored in the spine to protect and cushion it.
» We lose a cup of water a day from the soles of our feet and two to four cups through
breathing. » If you drink a can of cola a day you'll be consuming nearly 32,000
calories a year – switch to water and you'll knock off 4 kg without even trying.

5. Breakfast is best

It really is the most important meal of the day. I never, ever skip it, even on days when I have to leave the house at the crack of dawn for filming. Skipping breakfast will, over time, weaken your stomach and impair your digestive system. First thing in the morning your tummy is raring to go and your digestive enzyme juices are ready and waiting, so tuck in heartily with a big bowl of porridge oats, plenty of fresh seasonal fruit and some natural yoghurt.

Missing breakfast is an anti-ageing disaster

····⊰ It'll increase the likelihood that you'll binge in the afternoon and eat a large dinner because you'll be hit by an energy low. You'll be leaving yourself without the energy you need to get you through the day and instead consuming extra, wasted calories in the afternoon and evening.

····⊰ You'll actually be slowing down your metabolism – because your body has no food to draw energy from, it will slow down your metabolism to save energy.

····⊰ Your irregular daily eating pattern will lead to muscle loss as your body takes energy from elsewhere in the absence of food in the morning.

····⊰ Any good nutritionist will confirm that a high-fibre diet is one of the best ways to keep off weight, and breakfast provides the perfect opportunity to up your fibre intake. Choose high-fibre cereals and add some chopped fruit, or opt for wholemeal toast or one of the delicious seeded breads available these days.

DID YOU KNOW?
A low-fibre diet accelerates cellulite.

6. Call back carbs

I'm terrified by the number of people currently committed to carbohydrate-free diets. Carbs are essential for health and vitality; it's just a question of choosing the right ones. To stay youthful you need to have a slow, steady release of insulin into your bloodstream, so switch from eating over-processed, instant-buzz, highly refined carbs, such as cakes, sliced bread and biscuits, to slow-release carbs instead. Seeds, beans, wholemeal bread and vegetables will all work hard to keep you feeling young and fit.

Sleepless nights?

Eat carbs in the evening as they help to raise your serotonin levels and can encourage a good night's sleep, which is one of the best anti-agers there is. Avoid eating them throughout the day, though, or you could end up feeling tired and sleepy.

DID YOU KNOW?
Your diet should consist of about 60–65 per cent high-quality carbs, such as fruit, vegetables, and brown pasta, bread and rice.

7. Cut out coffee

I don't drink coffee at all. Caffeine raises levels of cortisol and insulin, which accelerate ageing, so try swapping that espresso for green tea. Drinking it just twice a day will help your body burn about 70 calories – that's enough to lose about half a stone a year. Research has shown that green tea contains antioxidants that speed up your metabolism. Not only that, this amazing drink can reduce the risk of heart disease and cancer and block the absorption of bad fats, which damage the skin by up to 30 per cent.

If you hate the taste of green tea, there are plenty of healthy alternatives. Peppermint tea is a fabulous, fresh-tasting drink that helps the digestive system. If you suffer from tummy aches, try it out. Nettle tea is rich in nutrients that are imperative for anti ageing. Sip some nettle tea once or twice a day and help beat that body clock.

DID YOU KNOW?
Claudia Schiffer is a fan of green tea – what more encouragement do you need?

8. Put the snack back

I never, ever graze between meals, not even on fruit. If you're eating three good meals a day you absolutely do not need to eat in between. Snacks are a vicious circle – they send blood-sugar levels soaring and moments later you're craving something else. Stop snacking and within a week you'll have completely lost your urge to eat between meals. If you find it hard not to snack, try to eat six smaller meals a day, but avoid eating rubbish. The more consistent your eating, the more routine your metabolism will become, which will help avoid drastic appetite swings.

9. Eat slowly and chew your food

I might sound like your mum, but these two simple rules are so important. Chewing helps to release food's nutrients, and it's only when saliva is released that the digestive process actually kicks in. It's common sense: chewing your food well stops your body having to work too hard breaking down great lumps of food. And eating slowly gives your brain a chance to realize when it's had enough – most people overeat because they bolt down their food so fast they're on to their second helping before they realize they're full. Eating should be enjoyable, so savour every mouthful.

10. Fat isn't always the bad guy

You need omega-3 and omega-6 oils (essential fatty acids) to stay looking young. These 'good fats' are found in lots of delicious foods, such as avocados, fish, seeds and lots of virgin oils. They're anti-inflammatory and help control the natural oil produced by the body, which keeps the skin soft, supple and young-looking. When you eat fats you kick-start your metabolism. Cutting them out is a disaster and is where many diets go wrong.

So there you have it: 10 easy ways to overhaul your diet and knock back the years. These are the rules I follow every day and they work for me, but that's just the start ... Eating the right foods can address specific problems that make us feel and look much older than we are, and the wrong foods can be incredibly ageing.

IS YOUR DIET AGEING YOU?

To find out just how much your diet is ageing you, take a look at these simple questions to discover which nutritional habits you need to overhaul:

1. What do you have for breakfast?
a. Porridge oats and fresh fruit
b. Cereal, toast and jam and a latte
c. Melon
d. Nothing, or just coffee
e. Rice crispies or cornflakes
f. Weetabix and milk

2. It's 11 a.m. and you're peckish. Do you fancy?
a. Some nuts
b. A biscuit or something sweet
c. Fresh fruit
d. Crisps and pork pie
e. A fruit smoothie
f. Nothing

3. Lunchtime. What do you opt for?
a. Baked potato with tuna and mayo, and a natural yoghurt
b. A cheese sandwich, can of cola and a chocolate bar
c. A green salad, reduced-fat dressing and water
d. Cheese and bacon salad with mayo and salad dressing and a white roll
e. Pine nut and basil potato salad
f. Blue cheese and pasta salad

4. You have a good friend coming for dinner, what do you cook?
a. Smoked salmon to start, followed by grilled fillet steak and vegetables
b. A take-away curry and a good bottle of red wine
c. Spaghetti with a simple tomato sauce and salad
d. Sausages, tinned potatoes and tinned vegetables
e. Stir-fry vegetables and potatoes
f. Chicken with ready-made sweet and sour sauce and a glass of wine

5. Drinks. What do you reach for when you're thirsty?
a. Water
b. Cola or fruit squash
c. Fruit juice
d. You don't get thirsty
e. Fruit drink
f. Coffee or tea

If you're mostly As, you can feel smug. You probably look pretty fabulous and almost certainly a good few years younger than you are. You're eating plenty of protein, but from all the right sources – nuts, seeds and vegetables. We need protein for all our body's tissues: it keeps muscles healthy and skin simply can't look good without it. A diet that lacks protein will be an ageing diet. Eat plenty of protein and you'll be in good company, as Demi Moore loves it. This diet gives you glossy hair and strong nails and, although you can't see it, your insides will be in pretty good shape too.

If you're mostly Bs, you need to take action now before you look 10 years older. Sorry, your diet is full of over-processed, sugar-ridden foods. I saw people on diets like this at my clinic all the time and they wondered why their skin looked dull and they were piling on the pounds. A common cry was, 'I don't have the energy I had when I was younger.' Is it any wonder? Throw out those processed foods and see the years fall away too.

> **DID YOU KNOW?**
> Sunflower seeds contain nearly as much protein as steak. » Parsley is an extraordinary herb. It has more vitamin C than oranges and enough B12 to make your energy levels soar.

If you're mostly Cs, I bet you're feeling pretty proud of yourself. You may think you're eating a really healthy anti-ageing diet, but I'm afraid I'm going to disillusion you. In fact, you're not getting enough nutritional value in your diet. You might be losing weight but your skin is probably ageing you and your hair won't be in tip-top youthful condition. By eating only fruit for breakfast you're not keeping your digestive system working at its best. Furthermore, your body needs protein and fat to keep its vitality – you're depriving it of the very foods it needs to fight ageing. I said at the beginning that looking 10 years younger isn't about dieting, it's about healthy eating. I want you to tuck into some porridge tomorrow morning!

If you're mostly Ds, your diet is packed with the worst types of fat. Do you think that by missing breakfast you're cutting down on your food intake and helping yourself stay slim? Well, you're not.

Breakfast is the most important meal of the day and is essential for getting your metabolism going. Yes, you're eating salad for lunch, but cheese and bacon are pretty high in fat. And don't forget that sausages and pork pies are some of the most high-fat foods in our supermarkets. Go for fish instead. It's an excellent anti-ageing food that will keep your brain lively too. That white roll has little to no nutritional value, so swap it for a wholemeal one, which will increase your fibre intake and provide you with some great anti-ageing nutrients.

With your high-fat, low-fibre diet you'll be putting on weight and, even more ageing, you'll be constipated and sluggish. That waste will sit inside you for far too long, and not only will it make you feel dreadful, it will make your skin look tired and dull. Eat more brown foods – have a high-fibre breakfast to start the day and get things moving.

If you're mostly Es, you're probably a vegetarian or vegan. Traditionally a vegetarian diet is perceived as supremely healthy, but you *must* maintain a good protein and dairy intake if you don't want to show signs of ageing. This diet appears to be the epitome of healthiness – low fat, no hard-to-digest meats and lots of salad and fruit. But you need something to replace those meats (and if you're a vegan, the dairy you're lacking too).

Start eating more nuts, pulses, wholegrain cereals, soya milk, dried fruit and dark green vegetables. Perhaps replace that tomato and basil salad at lunchtime with lentil soup, and instead of a fruit smoothie, have a yoghurt smoothie to increase your calcium intake (or a soya milk smoothie if you're vegan). Don't forget that low calcium results in osteoporosis.

When you're feeling thirsty, go for pure citrus fruit juice – the B vitamins, zinc and iron in vegetables are harder for your body to take up than those in meat, and you need vitamin C to help the body absorb them. Don't forget that zinc is a top anti-ageing mineral and will help your skin and hair look and feel great.

If you're mostly Fs, is your skin itchy? Your stomach bloated? This diet is healthy, but in my role as a dietician I've met many people whose diets are high in the foods that are known to cause allergies, and they really suffer as a result. Even the sweet and sour sauce is likely to contain monosodium glutamate, which is a powerful neuro-chemical that can result in headaches and other pains.

If this is a typical daily diet for you, and you're feeling sluggish, suffering from dry skin or eczema and getting a bloated stomach after you eat, it could be worth trying a detox diet and then gradually reintroducing first wheat, then dairy, etc, to see which is causing a reaction.

Coffee and tea are also known to cause problems for people who've developed food sensitivities. Try drinking water and herbal or fruit teas instead. Peppermint is particularly good for the digestion and could help stop bloating. Allergies and food sensitivity are likely to dry out your skin and contribute to early ageing in the form of wrinkles and fine lines. I have helped clients get their allergies under control and they've regained plump, youthful skin and seen their waistlines miraculously return.

AREAS FOR CONCERN

Many people who come to me look and feel much older than they are, but when I analyse why, I realize it's actually just one thing that's ageing them – weight gain, poor skin, awful hair, or simply lethargy.

If you can identify a specific problem area, it's almost certainly something that can be tackled or helped through diet. Here are some of the most common areas that give us cause for concern when it comes to looking and feeling old, along with some fabulous nutritional solutions to help target those age-old problems.

Skin

Your skin is probably the single biggest thing that determines how old you look. It's the largest organ in your body and one of the hardest working. It needs to be fed from within and deserves to be fed well. Cell turnover slows down in your 30s, and you'll naturally have less supple, radiant skin, so make sure your diet helps your skin restore these youthful qualities.

If your diet isn't right, you'll quickly look years older than you are. I'm not just talking about wrinkles here, but age spots, dry patches, uneven skin tone and blemishes, not to mention dull, sagging skin, blotchy pigmentation and ageing broken veins. Sun exposure is undoubtedly the skin's biggest enemy, but a poor diet isn't far behind. I can tell simply by looking at someone's skin if their diet's doing them no favours. However, the great news is that if your ageing appearance is down to eating the wrong foods, starting to eat well will quickly improve things.

Whatever your specific skin complaint, there are a few golden rules that will improve any complexion.

DID YOU KNOW?
Protein is great for your skin. If you don't have enough protein in your diet, you'll end up with rough skin and wrinkles, never mind poor muscle tone, brittle nails, a low libido and hair loss. A delicious organic chicken stir-fry cooked in sesame oil with added linseeds is a great skin-boosting meal.

Five skincare savers

1. Water

Yes, I know I've already banged on about this, but I make no apology for doing so again. Water is critical for healthy, hydrated, supple skin. It's easy, it's free and I promise you'll see fast results. As you age, you naturally produce less collagen, which helps restore elasticity and moisture retention, so help it along by drinking even more water.

2. Antioxidants

You need these in your diet as they slow down cellular ageing and fight the ageing free radicals your body produces in response to stress. They also help convert the naturally occurring amino acid tryptophan into brain-boosting serotonin, so you'll feel happier too. Fresh vegetables and most fruits are great sources of antioxidants. Antioxidants work better together than alone, and the most powerful ones contain beta carotene or vitamins A, C and E, which all help to turn back the clock.

VITAMIN C

Along with vitamins A and E, vitamin C fights cell-damaging free radicals, which reduce the elasticity of your skin's collagen and result in dry, rough skin. But remember, vitamin C doesn't hang around for long; it's water-soluble and short-lived in the body, so needs to be constantly replaced. In addition to eating vitamin C-rich foods, I always recommend taking slow-release vitamin C capsules, which work over an eight-hour period, giving your body more time to take advantage of it. Don't forget that vitamin C in foods is often destroyed or lost during cooking, which is why topping up with a supplement is important.

Top ten vitamin C foods:

⋯▷ Beans
⋯▷ Blackcurrants
⋯▷ Broccoli
⋯▷ Brussels sprouts
⋯▷ Cabbage
⋯▷ Cauliflower
⋯▷ Grapefruit
⋯▷ Oranges
⋯▷ Parsley
⋯▷ Strawberries

DID YOU KNOW?
Collagen is one of the main constituents of your skin, literally holding the body together, and is found in skin, tendons and bones. Vitamin C is essential for its production, so make sure you keep your diet well stocked with the wonder-vit for plump, youthful skin. » Reduce the time you cook potatoes and green vegetables. It'll make them tastier and they'll lose less vitamin C.

VITAMIN E

This is an amazing vitamin. It works alongside vitamin C, which protects vitamin E from being destroyed, so make sure you eat foods that contain both to get maximum benefit. Vitamin E is a warrior, fighting the free radicals that damage our cells and raising our immunity levels, so eat plenty of vitamin E-rich foods to feel young and healthy again.

Top ten vitamin E foods:

- ⟶ Almonds
- ⟶ Cereals
- ⟶ Hazelnuts
- ⟶ Margarine
- ⟶ Olive oil
- ⟶ Peanut butter
- ⟶ Prawns
- ⟶ Sunflower seeds
- ⟶ Sweet potatoes
- ⟶ Wheatgerm

BETA CAROTENE

Not only can this prevent ageing, it actually reverses many of the symptoms. We are probably only just beginning to understand its true powers – research is increasingly proving that beta carotene can prevent cancer and heart disease. Eating lots of beta carotene-rich spinach may reduce the risk of stroke by 40 per cent. Once in the body, beta carotene converts to vitamin A, which brings with it greater immunity against a host of illnesses. And if you have trouble remembering which foods are beta carotene rich, go for orange or yellow vegetables and you won't go far wrong.

Top ten beta carotene foods:

··⟩ Apricots

··⟩ Cantaloupe melon

··⟩ Chicory

··⟩ Mangos

··⟩ Pink grapefruit

··⟩ Pumpkin

··⟩ Raw carrots

··⟩ Spinach

··⟩ Squash

··⟩ Tomato juice

VITAMIN A

This is your skin's best friend. If you think your skin looks older than it should, increasing your vitamin A intake should be the first thing you do. Liver, fish-liver oil, whole milk, egg yolks, cheese and butter will all deliver a good dose of this fantastic vitamin, which helps prevent acne, dermatitis, rough and dry skin, and promotes healthy eyes.

Vitamin A is found in two forms: as retinol in foods from animal sources and as carotenoids in foods from plant sources, beta carotene being the most common. Beta carotene can be converted into retinol in the body, with 6 mg of beta carotene becoming the equivalent of 1 mg of retinol.

NOTE: Excess retinol can be toxic and may be dangerous for unborn children, so pregnant women, or those trying for a baby, are advised not to take high-dose vitamin A supplements unless they've been advised to do so by a health professional.

DID YOU KNOW?

Supplement your skin from inside and out. Make sure your moisturizer contains vitamins A, C and E in forms that can penetrate deep into your skin. Get scientific and look on the label for ascorbyl palmitate (vitamin C: a potent antioxidant and eradicator of toxic free radicals) and retinyl palmitate (vitamin A acetate: rejuvenates skin; accounts for about 80 per cent of the vitamin A found in the skin).

3. Silica

What do the earth's crust and your skin have in common? Both are packed full of silica, an element that has amazing anti-ageing properties. It increases the skin's elasticity; repairs brittle, cracked nails; helps the skin store moisture, thus reducing wrinkles and skin problems, and can even reduce grey hair.

SILICA-RICH FOODS:

- ⟶ Barley
- ⟶ Horsetail herb
- ⟶ Millet
- ⟶ Oats
- ⟶ Onions
- ⟶ Red beet
- ⟶ Whole wheat

4. Stop the salt

Or at least cut right back. Too much sodium will make your skin puffy, especially in vulnerable areas such as the delicate skin under your eyes. If you don't want that bag-lady look, say no to salt. Even if you've been used to high quantities of salt, you'll be amazed how quickly you can get used to a low-salt diet. Processed foods are full of it, so that's another good reason to wave goodbye to them, and there are a few foods that are obviously high in salt, such as sausages, hard cheese and bacon, so go easy on them. But be careful: there's hidden salt in all sorts of places that might not be obvious – bread, tinned soups and even breakfast cereals can contain alarmingly high amounts.

5. Help your insides and your skin will say thank you

Don't eat lots of processed food that will block up your system; stick with simple, fresh produce. Fried foods, fatty meat and refined dairy products all clog things up. Your skin is meant to excrete waste products, and if they can't get out, they'll build up, and that's when the spots and broken veins appear. Stopping eating 'clogging' foods will give you clearer skin.

Orange peel thighs?

Every woman's nightmare. Add some fibre to your diet to help combat the risk.

Avoid:
- Foods high in salt or sugar
- High-fat foods
- Refined foods
- Starchy foods
- Fatty meat
- Fast food
- Sugary drinks and alcohol
  (with the exception of red wine)

Banish cellulite with:
- Fibrous and low-fat foods
- Metabolism boosters such as water, pure fruit and vegetable juices and herbal or fruit teas
- Raw fruit and veg, wholemeal products and lean meat

DID YOU KNOW?
Scientists in the USA found that people who eat three apples a day lose weight. Apples are packed with fibre, which aids digestion and helps lower cholesterol. They're also great for banishing cellulite.

Problem skin

Food doesn't stay on the inside. Remember, what you eat today will show in your skin tomorrow. Take a look at the table below to see how to fix those worrying, and ageing, skin problems with some simple dietary changes.

	Dry skin	Oily skin	Puffy face and water retention	Rough skin
Probable dietary causes	Lack of essential fatty acids, dehydration and vitamin A deficiency	High-fat diet	Food allergies and lack of essential fatty acids. Also possible hormonal imbalances	Vitamin A deficiency, diet lacking in water and essential fatty acids
Cut down on sugar, alcohol, tea and coffee	✓	✓		
Increase water intake to 2 litres a day and eat moisture-rich foods	✓		✓	✓
Increase essential fatty acids found in seeds and their cold pressed oils	✓	✓	✓	✓
Cut down on saturated fats	✓	✓		
Supplements	Vitamins A and E, evening primrose, flax and borage oils, omega-3 and omega-6 fish oils	Vitamin C	Flax, evening primrose or borage oil, zinc, magnesium, biotin and vitamin B6, omega-3 and omega-6 fish oils	Vitamins A, C and E, zinc and selenium, evening primrose or borage oil. Boost your beta carotene with yellow, orange and red fruit and veg
Other solutions	Get allergy tested. Most GPs will refer you to someone who can do this			

Energy

I'm sure most of us envy children their energy – they never stop. Obviously as we get older our energy levels drop, but they don't need to. Think of food as fuel and simply fill up on the five-star stuff. Dietary changes can make an enormous difference to your stamina levels. Vitamin B is fantastic for restoring and balancing hormone levels, and vitamin B-rich foods will make you look and feel years younger. B12 is particularly important for combating fatigue, and is found in meat, eggs and dairy products, so it's not difficult to introduce plenty into your diet. Potassium is another great energy booster, so tuck into some oranges, bananas and peanut butter.

DID YOU KNOW?

In a study of 200 people, 70 per cent noticed emotional and health benefits when they upped the amount of fruit and veg in their diet. These fresh foods are a vital source of the nutrients that help us stay happy and balanced.

RELAX AND GET RID OF SPOTS

Oily skin can be caused by stress, which increases the stimulation of adrenalin in the body, leading to overproduction of sebum and thus oily skin. Take a pantothenic acid supplement and vitamin C to help counteract stress. Don't forget, having a little oil on your skin helps to keep the skin moisturized and prevent wrinkles.

Hair

A glossy mane of hair is instantly associated with youth, and just like dull skin, hair in poor condition has the ability to age you. I'm not just referring to an ageing hair*style*; how healthy your hair looks gives clues to your age and can easily make you look considerably older than you are. Hair that's greying, dull, brittle or balding can add years on to you, and yet so many of us put up with these ageing conditions unnecessarily. Banishing them is as simple as A, B, C – vitamins that is – so instead of forking out for expensive hair products, why not treat your hair from the inside and watch the years fall away.

1. **Drinking turns your hair grey**
   Alcohol drains the B vitamins from your system, which leads to premature greying. Boost those B vitamins and keep your colour.

   B-GROUP VITAMIN-RICH FOODS THAT HELP COMBAT GREYING
   ⋯⋗ Brewer's yeast
   ⋯⋗ Offal, particularly liver
   ⋯⋗ Raw wheatgerm
   ⋯⋗ Rice bran
   ⋯⋗ Water from cooking vegetables or brown rice
   ⋯⋗ Whole, unpolished brown rice

2. **Bees are good for your hair**
   Bee pollen is an amazing substance and contains massive amounts of the nutrients we need for cell growth. It can be taken as a supplement or in cosmetics to help prevent hair greying and boost hair condition. Royal jelly is also great for hair and is packed full of pantothenic acid and vitamin B5. Boost your diet with vitamin B5 if you've been taking antibiotics, sleeping pills or the contraceptive pill.

3. **Peanut butter stops you balding**
   Peanut butter contains a nutrient called inositol, which has been found to work against male hair loss.

4. **Dry, brittle hair? Boost those unsaturated fats**
   Unless you've been damaging your hair with bleaching or heat, it's possible that hair that's dried out or brittle is down to a lack of essential fats. Start sprinkling your meals with linseeds or sesame seeds, or cook in olive or macadamia oil – all excellent sources of 'good' fats.

5. **Fading fast**
   Loss of hair colour can be a sign of zinc deficiency. Maintaining your glossy colour is easy, as zinc can be found in numerous foods, including meat, fish, milk and egg yolks.

Nails

Have you ever seen a celebrity on the red carpet with dry, broken nails? No. Because healthy-looking nails are essential for giving a youthful impression. Don't allow your nails to let you down. Never mind a manicure; eat your way to Hollywood-healthy nails.

⋯⟫ White spots on your nails could indicate a zinc deficiency. Eat plenty of mushrooms, wheatgerm, meat or fish, or boost your diet with a good supplement.

⋯⟫ Nails are packed with silica, so if they're brittle and cracked, it's likely you need more silica-rich foods, such as whole wheat, onions and oats.

⋯⟫ For all-round nail beauty, sunflower seeds and oil are hard to beat – I like to sprinkle sunflower seeds over my cereal in the morning.

Weight

There are varying perspectives on weight and age, with some specialists saying that those with a lean physique have a longer life expectancy, while others have found that if you're over 75 and slightly overweight you're likely to live longer. However, it's easy to associate a healthy weight with youthfulness, so piling on the pounds can add years to your appearance. One of the most ageing problems I deal with in my clients is when they're overweight, as it's often a symptom of an all-round unhealthy diet. More importantly, keeping yourself at a size and weight you feel happy with does wonders for your self-esteem, which will instantly give you a youthful glow and positive attitude.

DID YOU KNOW?

When combined with pantothenic acid, PABA (para amino benzoic acid), which is similar to folic acid, has been found to reverse hair greying in animals. Could it help us in the same way? Try boosting your diet with whole grains, raw wheatgerm or offal.

COLOUR AND FOODS

I love to make sure that my meals are an artist's palette of colour. The natural colours in food are produced by the antioxidants and nutrients they contain – all of which are fabulous anti-agers that also fight illness and disease. Sticking to a diet containing vegetables in a limited colour range will limit the range of antioxidants and nutrients you take in, so you're likely to end up with the ageing signs of deficiency. Don't be confused, though. Going for a colourful diet doesn't mean that artificial colourings are good for you. What I'm talking about is the beautiful, natural rainbow of colours that Mother Nature has spread throughout the food world.

Try to include foods from the following five colour groups in your diet each day and you'll keep yourself defended against all the signs and problems of ageing.

'The beautiful is not always expensive, and the expensive is not always beautiful.'

ANON

Yellow, orange and red

This group contains antioxidants called carotenes. They protect the cells and membranes of your body – such as your skin and cell walls – and are vital for fighting the effects of ageing and protecting your body against stress, pollution, chemicals and the sun – all causes of the visible signs of ageing. These fruit and veg are also high in vitamin C, which we know is a great weapon in the war against colds and flu. And the carotenes present in them are anti-inflammatory, as well as being great for anti-ageing, will protect your nervous system and guard against cancer. As this group of foods is available all year round, there's no excuse not to eat them.

Yellow, orange and red foods:

- Bananas
- Carrots
- Corn
- Lemon
- Mango
- Oranges
- Peppers
- Pomegranates
- Squash
- Strawberries
- Tomatoes

DID YOU KNOW?
Pomegranates and their juice have become the favourites of the stars because of their excellent anti-ageing properties.

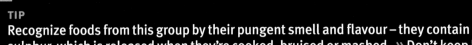

TIP
Recognize foods from this group by their pungent smell and flavour – they contain sulphur, which is released when they're cooked, bruised or mashed. » Don't keep herbs for too long – when their flavour starts to fade, so do their antioxidant properties.

DID YOU KNOW?
Avoid pre-bagged salads: many of their antioxidant properties are lost in the packaging and storage process.

Green

Green foods can actually help you lose weight.
They hold back the enzymes in your body that
raise your blood sugar and so prevent you from
craving unnecessary high-sugar, high-fat foods.
They're packed with nutrients such as selenium,
which is needed for your metabolism, boosts
your immune system, is an excellent antioxidant
and helps vitamin E to do its job. Green foods
are warriors against wrinkles and essential
parts of your anti-ageing lifestyle.

Green foods:

- Asparagus
- Broccoli
- Brussels sprouts
- Cabbage
- Chives
- Garlic
- Leeks
- Marjoram
- Onions
- Oregano
- Peppermint
- Rosemary
- Sage
- Tarragon
- Thyme

Purple and blue

Not only are purple and blue foods sweet and delicious, they're also great for your circulation, helping to improve the function of your heart, veins and arteries. They contain a group of antioxidants called flavonoids, which are major players in the anti-ageing game. They're also helpful in preventing and fighting allergies, and are natural antibiotics. Ironically, as many of the members of this group are so sweet, some purple and blue foods help fight tooth decay – green tea is great for this – and we all know how important a dazzling smile is for a youthful-looking face.

Purple and blue foods:

- Aubergine
- Beetroot
- Blackberries
- Blueberries
- Cranberries
- Cherries
- Pomegranates
- Red apples

- Grapes
- Green and black tea
- Juices of purple and blue fruits, including red and white wine
- Prunes
- Raspberries

DID YOU KNOW?
Don't peel aubergines as their skin has amazing properties and will protect you against heart disease and fight free radicals.

DID YOU KNOW?
Brown foods contain powerful anti-cancer fighters and help lower your cholesterol. » Processed white carbs have the opposite effect to their filling, brown alternatives: they actually increase your appetite by raising your blood-sugar levels.

Brown

These days, many of us aren't getting enough brown foods, yet they contain an array of anti-ageing nutrients. We seem to have got a taste for the white versions of staple carbs, such as bread, pasta and rice, which simply don't have the same goodness as their brown counterparts. Ditch the dazzling white and go back to a high-fibre, natural diet; it'll taste better and have far greater benefits than its over-processed white relatives. One of the most obvious functions of brown foods is in aiding digestion. They're packed full of healthy fibre, which keeps your bowels regular and prevents your system becoming sluggish – which in turn can lead to cellulite, dull skin and a distinct lack of energy. Brown foods are also rich in powerful B vitamins, vitamin E, zinc, magnesium and antioxidants. They are great 'fillers' – I always try to have some of this food group in my breakfast as they stop me feeling hungry and wanting to fill up on less nutritious foods before lunch.

Brown foods:

- Almonds
- Beans
- Brazil nuts
- Brown mushrooms
- Brown pasta
- Brown rice
- Cashews
- Chickpeas
- Couscous
- Flaxseeds
- Lentils
- Peanuts
- Poppy seeds
- Potatoes
- Sesame seeds
- Sunflower seeds
- Tofu
- Walnuts

...is essential for strong bones. Foods in this group also contain the marvellous, essential fat omega-3. The physical signs of omega-3 deficiency include dry skin and water retention, while a large deficiency can affect your memory and ability to learn. One of the best omega-3 sources is fish; if you aren't eating much fish then perhaps it's time to revisit the great British tradition of fish on Fridays. Eating these foods is also a great way to increase your anti-ageing vitamin A intake and boost your calcium levels.

DID YOU KNOW?
If you're getting enough iron from the rest of your diet, there's no need to eat red meat, as fish and eggs are excellent sources of protein, and there's a possibility that too much animal protein in your diet can make you prone to disease.

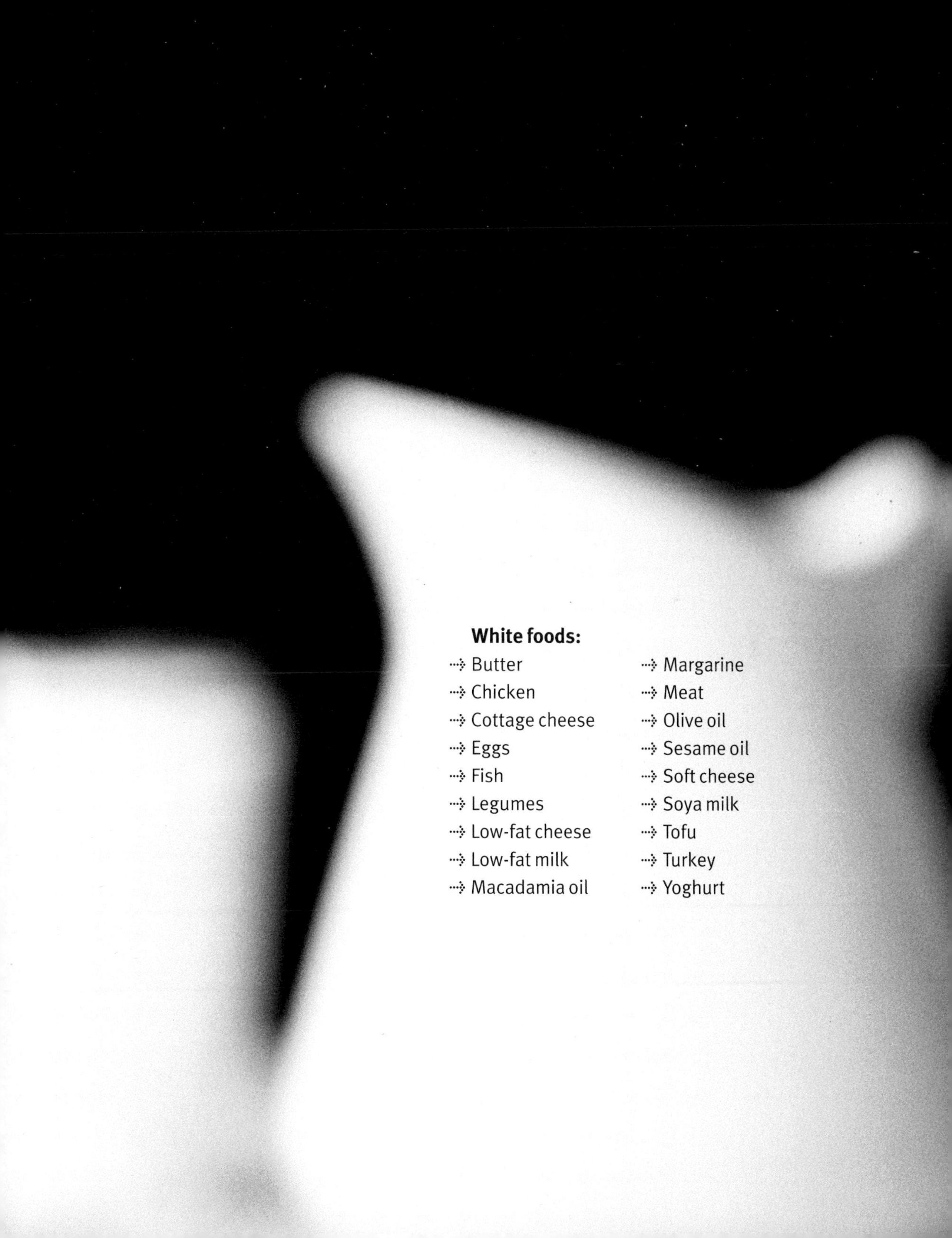

White foods:

- Butter
- Chicken
- Cottage cheese
- Eggs
- Fish
- Legumes
- Low-fat cheese
- Low-fat milk
- Macadamia oil
- Margarine
- Meat
- Olive oil
- Sesame oil
- Soft cheese
- Soya milk
- Tofu
- Turkey
- Yoghurt

DID YOU KNOW?
Prunes are the top-scoring ORAC food, followed by raisins. Drying plums and grapes removes the water that would otherwise dilute the antioxidants. » Just seven prunes a day gives your body all the antioxidants it needs.

WRINKLE-ZAPPING FOODS

Do they exist? Well, research is still theoretical, but early results from the Human Nutrition Research Centre in Boston suggest that eating high-ORAC fruits and vegetables may slow the signs of ageing. So what are ORAC foods? Oxygen Radical Absorbance Capacity, or ORAC, is a test to measure the levels of antioxidants present in food. In theory, these foods could halt the development of wrinkles, protect joints from arthritis, improve memory and maintain brain cells, and even reduce the risk of heart disease and some cancers.

Researchers have put together a table of the top scoring, wrinkle-zapping fruits and vegetables. Their high levels of antioxidants come from plant pigments called polyphenols. They are also rich in vitamins C and E, both powerful antioxidants, as well as containing folic acid, iron, antiseptics, antifungals and cholesterol-lowering properties. It's thought that the combination of nutrients in these foods makes them more effective than simply taking each nutrient alone or as a supplement.

ORAC-rich fruit & veg

- Alfalfa sprouts
- Aubergine
- Avocado
- Beetroot
- Blackberries
- Blueberries
- Broccoli
- Brussels sprouts
- Cherries
- Corn
- Garlic
- Kale
- Kiwi fruit
- Onions
- Oranges
- Pink grapefruit
- Plums
- Prunes
- Raisins
- Raspberries
- Red grapes
- Red peppers
- Spinach
- Strawberries

AGEING DIET

We've taken a look at the foods that will help you defy the signs of ageing and roll back the years, but what are you eating and drinking that's doing just the opposite and wrecking your skin with wrinkles and piling on ageing excess weight?

Alcohol

I can spot a heavy drinker a mile off: they usually have small broken capillaries around their face and unsightly, ageing blotches. Excessive alcohol consumption dehydrates your skin, which isn't a good look. It also puts a big strain on many of your internal organs, and if your liver isn't working efficiently, the build-up of toxins will wreak havoc with your skin. I expect that most of you could recognize the signs of over-consumption of alcohol in a person. However, even at a normal intake level, alcohol is one of the biggest contributors to premature ageing. It hinders your blood circulation, which shows up in your skin as wrinkles, burst blood vessels and pale, dull skin. However, a couple of glasses of red wine can be a great way to wind down, and red wine has positive antioxidant benefits, so can help the battle against ageing. Young red wines are the most beneficial, so pick these over wines that have been oak-aged for years.

If red wine isn't your drink of choice and you still want want to enjoy the occasional tipple, try these tips to counteract alcohol's negative affects:

- Drink lots of water to counterbalance the dehydrating effects of alcohol and flush it out of your system – this will also help prevent a hangover.
- Take a sauna – they're great for circulation and that great anti-ager, relaxation.
- Increase your intake of fruit and veg, as their antioxidants will protect you against alcohol's ageing properties.
- Take a high dose of vitamins C and B to help detoxify you.

Sugar

During my years as a dietician I've come to the conclusion that one of the most ageing foods is sugar, and yet many of our diets are packed full of it. It has a negative effect on your digestive system and can cause irritable bowel syndrome, resulting in painful bloating, depression, stomach cramps, migraines and sluggishness, all of which contribute to the obvious signs of ageing. Stuff yourself with sugar and your skin will be more likely to sag and wrinkle because sugar destroys your collagen production. Don't forget, though, that sugar isn't always obvious. Even white flour quickly turns into glucose. If you're not sure whether you're eating too much sugar, see if you're sleepy after meals. If you are, it's likely that you're suffering from sugar overdose and it's time to cut down.

If you aren't eating a balanced, healthy diet, your blood-sugar levels are likely to be all over the place, constantly dropping low so you crave sugar fixes, and then leaping to high levels where sugar ends up being stored as unnecessary fat. Many foods are packed with hidden sugars these days, so it can be difficult to keep track, but most people are eating high amounts of processed sugars, which release fats. However, if you're taking my advice and sticking to unprocessed foods, it shouldn't be too hard to stabilize your levels. Follow these tips to help you balance your body sugar and give your body a helping hand in looking and feeling more youthful.

⋯⇢ **Don't eat more than you need** It's easy to graze on chocolate, crisps, cakes and fizzy drinks, which are all high in sugar. Many of us eat huge portions at mealtimes – but remember, quality is much more important than quantity when it comes to keeping your sugar intake down.

⋯⇢ **Avoid processed foods** They're packed with sugar. If you really have to snack, eat a calcium-boosting natural yoghurt, fresh organic fruit, raw carrots and hummus or a smoothie. They'll satisfy your snack craving without increasing your blood-sugar levels.

⋯⇢ **Eat foods that keep your blood-sugar levels even** Foods that contain vitamins B3, B6 and C, zinc and chromium all help regulate your blood-sugar levels and burn fat.

⋯⇢ **Boost your diet with konjac fibre and HCA (hydroxycitric acid)** These can be bought in good health-food shops. Konjac fibre helps balance your blood sugar. HCA decreases your body's ability to make body fat from excess food you consume *and* reduces your appetite. However, supplements such as these only help if you're making overall dietary changes.

> **DID YOU KNOW?**
> The sweetest sugar is fructose, so satisfy your sweet tooth with fruits and honey for a natural alternative to processed sugars.

Rules to remember

I've told you about the good, the bad and the downright
ugly-making. You can't deny that it's not too hard to make
some small, simple changes that will really make an impact
on how young you look.

However, should this all seem a bit daunting, if you try nothing
else, remember these top five tips for youthful nutrition. Even
the little steps can take you a long way in the anti-ageing race:

⋯⋗ Drink more water.
⋯⋗ Eat more fresh fruits and vegetables.
⋯⋗ Cut right down on 'bad fats' and sugar.
⋯⋗ Eat more fibre.
⋯⋗ Eat food from all the colour groups to get a full range
   of anti-ageing nutrients.

DID YOU KNOW?
If you're under- or overweight your
body will take longer to process
alcohol. » Alcohol actually makes
you go to the toilet more and uses
up your body's water, so not only do
you need to drink enough water to
flush out the toxins, you need extra
to balance out the amount you lose
through urinating.

style & looking good

CHAPTER EIGHT

Anyone can buy the latest trends and appear fashionable, but looking stylish is something entirely different. With a little expertise and a healthy dose of confidence, it's possible to look effortlessly fantastic all the time. Finding the look that's right for you and ditching the dated style you loved a decade ago will not only boost your confidence but also help you shed the years.

I believe that the clothes you wear can say more about your age than the number of wrinkles on your face, and when it comes to guessing your age, after your face, the next thing people notice is how you dress. I meet people every day who don't have many wrinkles but dress like old women, so I immediately assume they're a decade older than they are. Before you even consider plastic surgery, I'd always suggest revamping your wardrobe. It's not only cheaper, but there are no adverse risks and you'll look and feel 10 years younger instantly. Trust me, it will be the best investment you've ever made.

In my experience as both a dietician and personal stylist, I find the secret to people feeling happier with the way they are usually lies in their self-esteem, not the number of wrinkles on their forehead. One of the reasons I decided to become a stylist was because of the powerful impact clothes can have on the way you feel and carry yourself. It's about giving you back control. Most of us get stuck in a rut at some point in our lives – perhaps you've gained some weight, nothing fits and everything is an effort. And being told you need to exercise and cut out chocolate, alcohol and cigarettes does nothing to lift your spirits.

I am passionate about the effect clothes can have on the way you feel about yourself and your body. I liken it to falling in love: when you fall in love, you automatically start to eat healthy foods, spend time thinking about what you're going to wear and go to the gym because life is good. You wake up with a spring in your step and a smile on your face – you simply feel more alive.

By the time you've finished reading this chapter I want you to feel alive. I want you to feel inspired to clear out your closets and re-evaluate your relationship with clothes.

I'm not suggesting you walk around in miniskirts and high heels all the time. On the contrary, if you want to look effortlessly stylish, you need to feel comfortable in your own skin, and that needn't be as complicated as you think. Adapting the latest trends, adding the right accessory to enhance your look is easy when you know how, and it's a sure way to regain that youthful spark and take years off your look.

So if everything I've mentioned in this book is too much to absorb right now, if there's only one thing you do – invest in some new clothes.

CLOTHES

A full wardrobe doesn't always mean having a vast choice of what to wear. Your wardrobe really should be a case of less is more. A few well-chosen outfits with accessories to update your look will last you through more than one season. Clothes should always match you and your lifestyle, including the colours and styles that suit you best.

It's all about realizing what works for you. There's no point in buying the latest must-have if you don't look good in it or, more importantly, *feel* good in it. There's also no point in buying something you love but know you're never going to wear. Everyone makes mistakes from time to time. Who hasn't got at least one embarrassing fashion disaster lurking somewhere in their wardrobe? The secret is not to hang on to them. Finding out what's right for you will make you feel more confident, happy and sexy – in fact, everything that goes towards making you look and feel 10 years younger.

So what's your biggest mistake? Don't worry, even I'm not perfect. I once spent £350 on a summer coat that I wore only once before it got bleached by the sun. It hung in my wardrobe for weeks on end and eventually it wasn't worth wearing at all. I still feel sick when I think about it, but not as bad as I did when it was still in my wardrobe, staring back at me every morning.

'Never fall for fashion, always be in style. Fashion fades, only style remains.'

COCO CHANEL, DESIGNER AND COUTURIER

Why we make mistakes

As we get older, our lifestyles, body shape and priorities change. Many of my clients are women who've swapped city careers for the school run. They have less time for themselves and have exchanged relaxed lunchtime browsing through the clothes rails to occasional, rushed shopping trips. Instead of knowing what's around and having a good idea of what they want to buy and where to find it, they suddenly haven't a clue. They've lost confidence in clothes and have a cluttered wardrobe full of old work suits they'll never wear again. and a comfort uniform of easy clothes they sling on as they rush to get their (perfectly dressed) children to school on time. Their idea of femininity and style has got lost somewhere amid the nappies and muslins. Then a few years down the line they feel frumpy, nothing fits or looks right, and they don't know where to begin.

Sound familiar? Then suddenly you get a wake-up call. You need clothes for a smart function and there's nothing inspiring in your wardrobe, so you rush off for an hour, or half a day's shopping. You haven't a clue what's out there or even what shops to go to, and the sizes that used to fit you no longer do. What used to look good doesn't work. Help! You're in a style rut.

TIP
Never have anything in your wardrobe that isn't either useful or beautiful.

Common mistakes

⋯⋗ **I'm a mum, I have to dress like one** You don't. Just because you're a mother doesn't mean it's a crime to look trendy and feel sexy. Frumpy looks old no matter what age you are. Even your children will feel proud to have a trendy mum picking them up from school. It's tough but true. Just because your partner and kids don't say anything doesn't mean they don't notice how you dress. Silence doesn't mean approval, just acceptance. Test it for yourself: buy something new and wait for the comments.

⋯⋗ **Throw out your 'fat' and 'thin' clothes** I'm not joking here – many of my clients have a selection of sizes, just in case. I tell them to get rid of them all. There's just no point. The fat clothes are a negative reminder and the thin clothes are depressing because they no longer fit. It's really important to feel good about yourself *now* and to choose clothes that work for you *now*. Weight is often a psychological battle rather than a physical one, so take out the psychology by wearing clothes that fit you properly as you are. That way, the minute you put on a kilo or two you'll feel it, which will give you the impetus you need to do something about it before the problem gets any worse.

⋯⋗ **Colourless clothes** We all do it. Blacks, whites, pastels – they're safe but boring and frumpy. People avoid wearing colour for fear of drawing attention to themselves, but introducing a splash of colour to your wardrobe is a sure-fire way to look 10 years younger.

⋯⋗ **Seeking safety in black** It's slimming and can be chic and sexy, but head-to-toe black is too much and can make you look bigger as the eye struggles to define your shape. It also drains the colour from your face as it absorbs light, making it an unflattering, ageing colour, especially if you're at all tired.

DID YOU KNOW?
Clothes are intimately tied up with our self-image and confidence. When we get it right we instantly feel prettier, slimmer, sexier and more powerful.

···⫸ **Comfort clothes** Now don't get me wrong, I'm not against comfort – in fact I'm all for it – but my idea of comfort isn't a wardrobe full of oversized jumpers and velour tracksuits. If that's all there is in your wardrobe (aside from your dated work clothes), you're never going to feel or look good. Elasticated waists encourage comfort eating and lazy habits, and I defy anyone to look good in them, trendy or not. As a rule, I allow my clients a maximum of *one* slobbing sweater, although I prefer even comfort clothes to be fitted and shaped.

···⫸ **Shapeless clothes** People hide inside their baggy fleeces or sweaters, convinced they're disguising big boobs, saggy tummies or wide thighs. But it's a complete fallacy: baggy clothes hang off the widest point of your body, whether it's your boobs, tummy or hips, and make you look that big all over.

···⫸ **No attention to detail** Without the extras, such as belts, shoes and handbags, even the best-chosen clothes can look dull and boring. It's accessories that individualize an outfit and make you look younger.

'The secret of staying young is to live honestly, eat slowly, and lie about your age.'

LUCILLE BALL, ACTRESS AND COMEDIAN

Take action

Now we've dealt with the mistakes – and I bet there's isn't one of us who doesn't recognize at least a couple of them – let's be more positive:

⋯⟩ Just because you have children and are a mother, you still have a right to feel sexy and feminine.
⋯⟩ Think about who you really are and remember how you used to look and feel. You have the rest of your life ahead of you, so make the present perfect, not the past.
⋯⟩ Clear out your closet, and be brutal about it. Ditch all the clothes that are no longer part of who you are and that don't make you feel confident.
⋯⟩ Follow the three easy steps on the following pages to help you build a wardrobe that really works for you.

'Sex appeal is 50 per cent what you've got and 50 per cent what people think you've got.'

SOPHIA LOREN, ACTRESS

Step 1: Clear out your wardrobe

⇢ Set aside three hours when you're free from any other commitments. Switch on the answering machine and turn off your mobile. Put on a favourite CD – something upbeat and energizing. Make sure you have a full-length mirror and enough natural light, and a roll of bin liners for the cull. Now get to work.

⇢ Label four bin liners 'charity', 'alterations', 'rubbish' and 'storage'.

⇢ Start off by sorting all your clothes, putting like items together, such as trousers or shirts. Work systematically through each section.

Try on each item and take a long, hard look at yourself in the mirror. Ask yourself:

⇢ Does it make you feel good? If not – charity bag.
⇢ Do I actually like it? If not – charity bag.
⇢ Does it fit properly? If not – charity bag.
⇢ Does it require altering to make it fit properly or to update it for this season? If yes – alterations bag.
⇢ How many times did you wear it last season? If less than five times, it probably won't get an airing this season so give it to charity.
⇢ Is it worn, torn or covered in stains that will never come out? If yes – rubbish bag.
⇢ Does it make you look good? If not – charity bag.

⇢ Only the items that make you look good and feel good should go back in your wardrobe. Anything you're hesitant to get rid of should go into storage for six months. If during that time you don't think about them, give them to charity without going through the bags all over again.

⇢ Don't forget to go through your shoes, coats, accessories and underwear, too.

⇢ Take the charity bags to your nearest charity shop and the alterations bag to your nearest tailor.

Your wardrobe should now look a lot more streamlined. Well done, you're probably feeling shattered, but hopefully invigorated and energized too. For future reference, do this at the beginning of every season. The more often you do it, the quicker the process is. I cull my wardrobe at least twice a year, before I buy anything new for the following season. It helps me formulate ideas about the look I want and the pieces I need to achieve it. Having a streamlined wardrobe will enable you to get more out of what you already have. We often wear the same clothes all the time because we can't see the wood for the trees when we open our wardrobe doors.

Step 2: Build up a wardrobe

⋯⋗ The cupboard's now bare, so how do you start rebuilding a useful, complete wardrobe? A clever wardrobe doesn't require lots of effort. You need clothes that are the right shape and colour, with a mix of easy-to-wear accessories that will lift and update your outfits.

⋯⋗ Look carefully at what clothes you *need* and *can* wear. You need to critically evaluate what you already have and identify where the gaps are. It may be glaringly obvious, but it's often more subtle. The easy way to do it is to put outfits together. For example, you may have a red top, but nothing to wear it with, so perhaps you need a new pair of jeans or black trousers to go with it. Write a focused list that you can take shopping – think about trousers, skirts, dresses, jackets and coats for everyday wear as well as evening. And don't forget accessories.

⋯⋗ While doing this, note down all your outfit options on a separate piece of paper to serve as a quick reference when you're in a fix in the morning. If you struggle to mix and match the clothes in your wardrobe, it's always worthwhile getting expert advice from a personal stylist. The money you spend on the consultation, you'll save on your shopping spree, as you'll get more out of what you already have without the 'mistake' buys.

BEFORE YOU BUY ANYTHING THINK ABOUT:

⋯⋗ Who you are
⋯⋗ Your lifestyle
⋯⋗ The work you do
⋯⋗ Your day-to-day life
⋯⋗ Your leisure activities
⋯⋗ What you want
⋯⋗ What you need
⋯⋗ Clothes that are practical for you

Take time to look at fashion magazines to see what's available and what you like. This can be done on a train or tube, or while waiting for the kids to come out of school. I've already said I'm a great believer in style, but you don't have to dismiss fashion. It can often be practical and can add a certain pizzazz to your look that's unique, flattering and youthful.

TIP

For a wardrobe to work easily for you, clothes have to go together. There's no point in buying the perfect skirt if you have no tops, jackets or shoes to go with it. Think in terms of outfits and mixing and matching.

Step 3: Be your own personal shopper

Believe it or not, most women hate shopping.
It's hard to believe, I know, but every day
I hear, 'I don't know where to start', 'I feel
overwhelmed with choice and come home
empty-handed', or 'I never have time to shop,
so I end up buying a whole lot of stuff that
I never wear'. Read the tips on the following
page to learn how to shop like a professional.

TIP
**Only buy a piece of clothing
if it will go with at least two
items in your wardrobe.**

My top ten tips for successful shopping

1. Before you even leave the house make a list of exactly what you're looking for. Shops are designed to tempt you into buying what you don't need, so be vigilant and stick to the list.

2. Wear comfortable shoes, but if you're looking for clothes that you're likely to wear with heels, take a pair with you to try on. That way you can be sure that trouser and skirt lengths will work when you get them home.

3. The right bra will make a huge difference to how a top or jacket fits, so take along a couple of different styles. A push-up bra for eveningwear and a skin-tone T-shirt bra for light colours and fitted clothes are good choices.

4. Leave your partner at home, and remember, even your best friend isn't necessarily your best asset. Always trust your gut instinct. It's better to shop on your own or with a professional.

5. Even the most fabulous outfit will look terrible if the fit is wrong. Make sure that seams don't pull, that trousers cover the arch of your foot when you have shoes on, and that sleeves reach just over your wrist bone. Other pitfalls are buttons that pull across the bust, skirts that sit higher at the back and tummy rolls over the top of waistbands.

6. Take whole outfits into the changing room, even if you're only looking for one piece – it's easier to get the overall picture if the accessories are right.

7. Forget the size label. Every shop sizes slightly differently, so you may find you're a 12 in one and a 16 in another. Always take your usual size and one smaller into the changing room; often the smaller size will look better.

8. Do not let the sales assistant bully you into purchasing anything. Remember, it's in her interest to make a *sale*, but not necessarily to make you look good.

9. If you're not sure about a particular item, go home and think about it. If you can't get it out of your head after a week or two, go and get it.

10. Always ask about the store's returns policy before buying. If a store doesn't offer a full refund within a time limit, make sure you're 100 per cent certain before parting with your hard-earned dosh.

DID YOU KNOW?
Shopping burns over 200 calories an hour.

My tips for youthful style

1. The power of colour

Colour can really lift your mood, especially when it's dark and grey outside. And as we get older, wearing colour is even more important. We lose pigment from our skin as we age, so wearing colour near your face is a great way to subtly put colour back into your complexion without using make-up. Black may be slimming, but it's also ageing and it isn't easy for everyone to wear. I can only get away with a black polo neck if I really work hard on my make-up.

If you're still set on wearing that black top or jacket, coloured accessories are a great way of putting colour against your face and lifting the effect.

Work out what colours flatter you

Hold different colours up to your face in natural light. Be honest as you look in the mirror. Some colours flatter your skin, giving you a healthy glow and radiance; others have the opposite effect, draining your natural tone and making you look sallow or tired. Certain colours may even clash with your complexion. You'll soon recognize what works and what doesn't.

We tend to associate colour with young people because they often wear bright, fresh colours. A real sign that an adult has lost confidence in themselves is when they stop wearing colourful clothes.

Go for colour

Wear at least one piece of colour and put it where you want to draw attention. It might be the red shoes with the black trousers and top, or the pink handbag. Colour can work for you, diverting the eye away from all the bits you'd rather hide. Placed strategically, it draws the eye to where you want focus and accentuates your best features. Used cleverly, colour looks expensive and makes you more distinctive. Think Italian.

Colour to disguise

⋯⇥ If you have big thighs, wear a dark colour (black works well) on the bottom half and keep the brighter colours for your top .

⋯⇥ If you want to hide a big tummy, keep the darker colour for your top half.

⋯⇥ Big boobs and a less-than-flat tummy mean that the bright red top you love is not a good idea. But you could wear a black top with a red jacket over it. That way you get to keep the colour you like next to your face while drawing attention away from any extra flab.

> DID YOU KNOW?
> **Bold patterns can draw attention to features you'd rather hide.**

2. Show off your shape

⋯⋗ Fitted is always better. Anything baggy or square just hangs from the widest point and makes you look big all over. Don't be afraid to show your shape. Fitted clothes take years, and kilos, off the way you look – it may feel odd at first, but trust me, it works.

⋯⋗ A tailored jacket that goes in at the waist will give the illusion of shape and a defined waist even if you don't have one.

⋯⋗ Another common mistake is to go for clothes that are too big for you. Next time you're in a fitting room, take the size you think you are and one smaller. I'm not advocating skin-tight, which is never flattering, but make sure clothes fit properly. Often the bigger size looks OK, when the smaller size looks amazing. As the sizing in stores is never consistent, you may think you're a 14 when in fact you're a 12. Now that's an easy way to lose a dress size. All of us suffer from an element of body dysmorphia, where we think we're bigger than we are. One of my clients thought she was a size 14 when in fact she was a 10. She was too scared to try a smaller size in case it didn't fit, but when she did it completely changed her life.

⋯⋗ Also take note of where clothes end. The same top can make you look fantastic at one length but shapeless or hippy at another.

3. Fashion shapes

⋯⋗ Styles and shapes change – fashion constantly revives looks and fabrics, but often with subtle differences. Reading through fashion magazines will give you a good idea of the trends before you venture out shopping.

⋯⋗ Don't make the mistake of thinking that because a fabric is in vogue again, old garments you've held on to will still work. Check the shapes, lengths, detailing of buttons, sleeves and lapels. If they're not right, you'll just end up looking dated and it will be obvious you're wearing something you've hung on to for years.

⋯⋗ Vintage may be big at the moment, but it needs to be chosen well and carefully blended with modern clothes, otherwise you'll look like you've dressed straight out of a second-hand shop. If you're not a confident dresser, avoid high-fashion trends and opt for small tweaks to your wardrobe here and there, introducing new shapes, patterns and accessories.

⋯⋗ Some clothes are frumpy when worn by anyone older than 25, so don't make the mistake of thinking you'll look young simply because it's trendy. If it's not you, you'll look like a fashion victim instead of a fashionista. A perfect example is the twinset and pearls: charming at 20, frumpy at 30.

4. Dressing for your shape

If you have big boobs

⋯⟩ First stop – get yourself professionally measured for a well-fitting bra. This is absolutely essential and will make a lot of difference to the clothes you wear on top.

⋯⟩ Choose V-necks or wide scooped necklines as they give definition and are more flattering.

⋯⟩ Jackets and coats shouldn't button up to the neck if you want to avoid looking bulky and shapeless.

⋯⟩ Tailored jackets and coats without belts are the best choices.

⋯⟩ High-necks and, in particular, polo necks, are out I'm afraid. You'll end up looking as though you have no neck and are just big. You want to emphasize those sexy curves without adding bulk.

⋯⟩ For the same reason, avoid heavy wool sweaters. Fine knits are more flattering, especially if you go for cardigans or wraps.

⋯⟩ Avoid big, bold patterns on top.

⋯⟩ Tailored shirts can be flattering, but make sure the buttons don't bulge over your cleavage.

Heavy legs

⋯⟩ Try boot-cut trousers to give the illusion of curves.

⋯⟩ Long flares are also a good option as they hide any heaviness.

⋯⟩ Cropped trousers draw attention to your ankles and will not be flattering.

⋯⟩ Make sure trousers aren't too tight on your hips and thighs.

⋯⟩ Skirts are often more flattering than trousers as they disguise the thickness of your thighs.

⋯⟩ Skirts worn with long boots can disguise heavy legs and create a longer, leaner shape.

⋯⟩ A-line skirts are often the most flattering cut.

⋯⟩ The length of your skirts, dresses and coats is important. A wider skirt ending just below the knee will make your legs look slimmer by comparison.

⋯⟩ Avoid anything that ends on your calf as this is the widest part of your lower leg and can make you look frumpy.

⋯⟩ Invest in a variety of boots as they'll cover a multitude of sins, but always make sure your skirt covers the top of your boots and avoid showing your knees where possible.

⋯⟩ Flimsy fabrics will highlight any bulges. Fitted, thicker material is more flattering.

Pear shapes

- Avoid any tops, jumpers or jackets that cut across the widest point on your thighs.
- If you have a slim torso, a fitted top that skims your hips will emphasize your slim waist and draw attention away from your thighs. A good guide for length is that no top should finish more than four finger widths below your waistband.
- Three-quarter-length coats and jackets create a smooth outline, skimming over your thighs.
- Avoid jackets that end at your bum as they will emphasize its width. The idea is to break up your hip area, so cropped jackets that end just above or below the widest point on your thighs will be the most flattering.
- Fitted A-line skirts are flattering and make the most of your curves.
- Bias-cut skirts and dresses can be flattering depending on your height. If you're very short, the bias cut will emphasize your thighs. If you're 5' 6" or above, the bias cut can be flattering as it shows off your curves. Always wear a good pair of heels to lengthen proportions.
- Boot-cut trousers are definitely the way to go as they help balance your proportions. They're especially flattering when worn long over heels as they lengthen your legs.

- Never go for wide-leg trousers. You might think they'll disguise any bulk, but instead they'll sit on your thighs at the widest point and make you look shapeless.
- Cropped trousers should be approached with caution. If your legs are quite short, they're probably not for you. Don't choose a wide-leg shape as it will make you look wider. A dark colour worn with the same colour boots will be slimming and will visually extend the length of your legs.
- Think about the neckline you choose. A wide slash neck will balance out the width of your hips.
- Choose fabrics carefully. Silks and satins are gorgeous but they tend to cling in all the wrong places. The thicker and stretchier the fabric, the more flattering it will be.
- Dark colours help to disguise hips.
- Avoid pastels or white as they reflect light, thereby attracting attention to your hips.

If you're worried about a flabby tummy

⋯▸ Tops should still be fitted at the waist and worn out, not tucked in.

⋯▸ Avoid stretchy material or anything made with Lycra as it will cling in all the wrong places. If you do wear stretchy tops, always wear a jacket to hide lumps and bumps.

⋯▸ Avoid tops that are too short or reveal your midriff.

⋯▸ Ruching can be flattering and disguise any flab as it's impossible to tell what's you and what's material.

⋯▸ Wrap tops and dresses are another good choice for camouflaging your tum.

⋯▸ V-neck tops or sweaters worn with a shaped jacket over them give a curvy, flattering silhouette.

⋯▸ Long scarves hanging over your front focus attention away from what's underneath.

⋯▸ Always avoid high-waisted trousers as they will make your tummy look enormous.

⋯▸ Never wear elasticated waists as they add bulk.

⋯▸ Trousers should always be low waisted and not too tight. But avoid anything too low on the hips as it will leave everything hanging loose.

⋯▸ Flat-fronted trousers with a side zip are a good choice as they don't add any detail or bulk at the front.

⋯▸ Trousers with a wider waistband are also flattering.

⋯▸ Bias-cut skirts create a sexy hourglass shape and disguise your lack of waist.

⋯▸ Coats should be shaped at the waist, but avoid belts and double-breasted styles.

Saggy arms

⋯▸ These are a major area of concern for thousands of women in the UK, and are a problem associated with ageing.

⋯▸ Thin straps, sleeveless vests and cap sleeves should all be given a wide berth.

⋯▸ Instead opt for three-quarter-length, fluted and long sleeves.

⋯▸ Draw attention to your wrists. These invariably remain slim and can be an attractive feature. Choose pretty, delicate bracelets and coloured gloves.

TIP
Some fashions can be ageing. Jeans help to tone down a look and make it appear younger. Tweeds and pearls, for instance, don't look frumpy when worn with jeans.

5. Youthful wardrobe essentials

Jeans

I know jeans are trousers and many of the same rules for shape apply, but they are such a wardrobe staple that I thought they deserved their own section.

Jeans have been the uniform of youth since the 1950s and no wardrobe is complete without at least one pair. They are probably the most versatile item of clothing. Depending on what you put with them, they will take you from day to night time, work to weekend. Dress them down with trainers and a sweater or glam them up with a tuxedo jacket and heels. If you're going to spend money on anything, always opt for a good pair of jeans. You'll wear them all the time, they'll last longer and they'll always look good. Every time you put them on you'll feel great, and that's a sure way of looking younger. Sometimes we need a boost when we're having a 'fat day' and a good pair of jeans will always do the trick. Never compromise, you'll end up with a cupboard full of jeans you never wear. Spend a little time and money and they'll be your friend for life.

Always wash jeans inside out to preserve their colour and never tumble-dry them as they'll shrink. Don't use fabric softener with stretch jeans as it will ruin the fabric.

- High-waisted jeans will emphasize your bottom and tummy. Go for low-slung waistlines, which cover enough but visually halve the size of your bum.
- Tapered legs are only flattering on the slimmest, most petite hips and legs – whatever your age.
- For most mortals, boot-cut styles are kinder.
- Wear with heels to lengthen and slim the appearance of your legs and to dress up for evenings.
- Dark jeans tend to be smarter and more slimming.
- Cropped jeans are another popular option, but they can make your legs look shorter. If your legs are too big to carry off the jeans-tucked-into-boots look, opt for a pair of cropped ones and wear them with long boots.
- When wearing cropped jeans, make sure they always end just below your knee or at the bottom of your calf, otherwise you'll visually cut off your legs at the widest point.
- The thicker the denim, the slimmer you'll look, as the fabric will control you, not the other way around.
- Choose denim with some stretch. Your jeans will keep their shape better and they'll be much more comfortable to wear.
- Have one pair of shorter jeans to wear with trainers and one longer pair to wear with heels.

Coats and jackets

No matter what your clothes are like underneath, for a large portion of the year in the UK, the first and sometimes only thing other people see you wearing is your coat or jacket. The right coat can be thrown on over anything and will instantly make you feel fabulous. A jacket can pull a whole outfit together, but it can just as easily do the opposite and ruin your look. Coats and jackets are obviously functional, but that doesn't mean they can't also be fun, fashionable and stylish. They're a really important part of our wardrobe and yet many people make do with one useful but boring overcoat that they expect to go with everything. Coats used to be expensive, and of course it's still possible to pay a lot for one, but there are plenty of affordable, fashionable options available now, enabling you to invest in a couple each season.

DID YOU KNOW?

You don't always have to be able to close a jacket. Worn open, a jacket is often more slimming and emphasizes your waist. What a jacket looks like open is more important than what it looks like closed. A smaller size will hold its shape better, and you can accessorize with a scarf for warmth and colour.

Think about colours and what you want to wear a coat or jacket over. It's useful to have a choice of styles and lengths that work with your body shape and the clothes you wear.

- Three-quarter-length coats are a flattering choice, gliding over a multitude of bulges. They also look very *now*.
- If you're tall, a full-length coat can make a dramatic style statement, but if you're short, a full-length coat will make you appear smaller.
- Shaped, fitted jackets are a great way of giving yourself a waist and figure.
- Fitted shouldn't mean tight. Jackets should be shapely but not so tight that they highlight bulges.
- Fitted doesn't have to mean smart. Colour, choice of fabric and what you wear with it all contribute to the overall effect and you can dress it up or down as you wish.
- When choosing a jacket or coat, consider the length and fit carefully. Look at yourself from all angles and be critical: a few centimetres too long or short and it can both add kilos *and* years.
- Choose colour carefully. Remember, it's going to be next to your face on the drabbest, greyest of days, so make sure it flatters your skin tone.

Accessories

I've already touched on the importance of accessories, but for me they're simply essential. They are the best way of introducing individuality into your wardrobe and an easy way to update it and make you look more youthful. This is where you can have fun and be outrageous if you want to. Accessories don't have to be expensive, so you can afford to be adventurous and throw them out next season. This is one area where there's no need to play safe.

Collect pieces you like as you see them. Use accessories to bring your wardrobe up to date and to introduce colour and focus. Attention to detail makes all the difference between nice clothes and style. Accessories are also a great way of making you look more youthful. A new pink belt with jeans and last year's T-shirt immediately looks more funky and fun.

BELTS

These are my favourite accessory. They can change the tone of what you're wearing and give a whole new look to a one-colour outfit. Generally, narrow belts look better on narrow waists. Belts are a fantastic way to divert the eye away from a problem tummy. Wearing a belt on your hips instead of your waist, or positioning the buckle off-centre will all help to draw attention towards the belt and away from your lumps and bumps. Corset-style belts can also be used to cinch in the waist.

Belts have come a long way from being purely functional, where they simply hold up your trousers. They can add colour, detail, interest and focus, as well as dressing clothes up or down as you fancy.

DID YOU KNOW?
A wide belt around the hips will make your waist look smaller and disguise any flab on your stomach.

TIP
Add new accessories to last season's favourites to instantly update them.

BAGS

Bags can be classic and last for ever, or bold, brash and disposable. You really don't need to be subtle and can be as hip and up to the minute as you please. Use them as a statement or to match what you're wearing. There are lots around and they're not all expensive.

Again, don't make the mistake of investing in one bag that needs to fulfil a multitude of tasks. A large hold-all is ageing and can drag down an outfit and your posture. Assess the contents of your handbag and only carry around the bare essentials.

SCARVES

Scarves can add glamour and lend colour to your face on a dreary winter's day, cheer you up with a cute pattern when it's raining and help you cover up when necessary. You can never, ever have too many. Choose a variety of textures, fabrics and colours to see you through every mood and occasion.

JEWELLERY

Jewellery no longer has to be genuine; in fact, funky, individual costume pieces are much more youthful and fashionable. It doesn't have to cost a fortune, either, so you can afford to ring the changes.

Use bracelets, necklaces and earrings in jewelled colours and interesting designs to draw attention. They're another good way of introducing colour where you want it.

> **TIP**
> Drop earrings can lengthen short necks as they draw the eye along the whole length and up to the earlobe.

> **DID YOU KNOW?**
> Scarves are also a sure way to look frumpy. Fabrics and styles are ever changing, so last season's classic may not be chic this season. » Pair a light woollen scarf with a summer T-shirt to take you through that in-between stage from summer to autumn when it's not really that cold but summer clothes no longer look quite right. » Scarves can also double as belts, worn over the hips or through the loops in your trousers. » Winter scarves are a fantastic way to introduce colour and warmth to your wardrobe. Be bold and invest in at least three.

Shoes

I've watched it happen to people. As they get older, their choice of footwear gets ever more practical and frumpy. The need for comfort supersedes every other consideration and they forget just how sexy those killer stilettos used to make them feel.

Let me say it now: practical does not have to be frumpy. A good pair of trainers, flat boots, funky wellies or even ballet pumps are all comfortable, but they still have style and look fashionable. They'll be just as practical for walking the dog or taking the kids to school, but they'll actually look attractive and make you look youthful.

FEET FIRST

⋯⋗ Heels alter the way you stand. You can't slouch and you can't stomp.
⋯⋗ There's nothing like a pair of heels to make your legs look longer and leaner. Even the lowest heel can make a difference to your proportions.
⋯⋗ Boots are a great way to take denim and summer skirts through to autumn.
⋯⋗ Boots cover numerous imperfections and are a vital part of a winter wardrobe .
⋯⋗ Choose flat boots for every day and heels when you want to look more glamorous.
⋯⋗ Team knee-length boots with cropped trousers and skirts of any length for foolproof style.

IF YOU HAVE CHUNKY CALVES OR THICK ANKLES:

⋯⋗ Wedges help make chunky calves to appear slimmer.
⋯⋗ Open toes make ankles seem more slender
⋯⋗ Knee-length boots will cover everything, but avoid ankle-length boots (except under trousers).
⋯⋗ Avoid narrow, pointed toes; they're elegant but will make thick ankles and calves look even bigger.
⋯⋗ Avoid wearing shoes with ankle straps as they draw attention to your ankles and cut your leg in half.
⋯⋗ Avoid thick, chunky heels as they add bulk to your leg and foot.

TIP

If you can't face stilettos or high heels, try kitten heels. They'll have the same effect but are much easier to walk and run in.

When to spend and when to save?

I love a bargain and most of my clothes are simple and inexpensive. As far as economizing goes, I don't really think there are any hard and fast rules. Fashion and style generally cover a much broader spectrum than they used to.

If you can, it's worth splashing out on something more expensive if you really love it, it's classic and is something that will make you feel fantastic every time you wear it.

A good guide is to ask yourself, can I throw it over jeans and still feel fab? And will it last? If the answers are yes, then go ahead and splurge. Just make sure you enjoy it and don't feel too guilty. I would say, though, before you make a splash purchase, go home and think about it for a day or two. If you just can't get the item out of your mind, go back and buy it. If you don't give it a second thought, it wasn't that great after all.

TIP
Never, ever buy something for the sake of a bargain. I don't care if it's a designer item, only buy clothes that fit properly and, more importantly, that make you look and feel good, whatever the price. Otherwise it's false economy and you'll never wear it.

'I've been noticing gravity since I was very young.'

CAMERON DIAZ, ACTRESS

6. Caring for your wardrobe

It goes without saying that if you don't look your age, you certainly don't want your clothes to. Nothing ages clothing faster than not being properly cared for.

⇢ Always read the care labels and hand-wash or dry clean where appropriate.

⇢ Invest in a clothes brush and one of those nifty gadgets for debobbling sweaters.

⇢ Always separate white and coloured garments before washing them.

⇢ Use washing powder or liquid specially formulated for coloured clothes.

⇢ You'll get a much smoother finish if you iron clothes when they're still a little damp rather than waiting until they're bone dry. It's easier too.

⇢ Clean, well-pressed clothes should always be hung up or neatly folded, never crammed in.

⇢ Never tumble dry your clothes or underwear. They'll shrink and lose shape and they'll wear out faster. The tumble dryer should only be used for towels and sheets.

⇢ Dry clean items such as coats at the end of the winter before you put them away.

⇢ Put shoe trees in your shoes and boots – they'll keep their shape much better.

⇢ Reheel and resole shoes as soon as they're worn, don't let them wear down too far.

⇢ Polish leathers regularly.

⇢ Use a waterproof and stain-protector spray on suede and fine leather.

⇢ Store winter coats and jackets in separate clothing bags to prevent dust collecting on collars and to keep them fresh.

⇢ Always air clothes after a night on the town, before putting them back in the cupboard.

TIP
I'm all for clean clothes, but don't overwash or dry clean them too frequently. You'll simply wear them out faster.

the plans

CHAPTER NINE

the 24-hour plan

It's Friday evening – in just 24 hours you need to look fabulous for the party of the decade, but, despite your best intentions, you've done nothing to prepare. Your skin looks dull, your hair is lank and you could pack most of your wardrobe into the bags under your eyes. Help! Where's a fairy godmother when you need one?

Relax. You don't need magic. Just follow a few simple steps and, while you probably need a little longer than one day to look 10 years younger, there's no reason why you shouldn't look and feel stunning. Whatever you do, don't make the mistake of thinking there's not enough time. If you do, you'll just end up doing nothing.

The first step is to decide to make time for yourself. Forget the chores, at least for tonight and tomorrow and, most importantly, don't feel guilty about it. Women in particular get very used to putting others first, which is admirable, but it's important to look after yourself, too, because sometimes looking after yourself is the best way of taking care of others.

The night before

···› Ditch the planned takeaway and the idea of drowning your sorrows. What you need is an early night and a good night's sleep. And this evening you're going to do everything you can to make sure you get one. To do that, avoid caffeine and alcohol, which will disturb your sleep and leave you dehydrated. Instead, eat a simple supper, preferably high in carbohydrates, like pasta, which will help you sleep. If you add a tomato-based sauce and some broccoli, you'll also be adding essential vitamins and minerals. Try to eat at least two hours before you plan to go to bed as no one sleeps well on a full stomach.

···› Pamper yourself. Run a bath, add candles for atmosphere and pour in a measure of your favourite bath cream, or add a few drops of aromatic oil. Lavender, chamomile, jasmine and neroli are all calming, smell delicious and will help you relax and sleep better.

···› The bath is the ideal place to shave your legs and underarms. Don't wait until you've had a long soak as your hairs will be too soft and you won't get a smooth result. After five minutes is ideal, and the warm bath water should reduce any irritation.

···› If arms and shoulders that have been covered for weeks are suddenly going to be on display, a fake tan could be a good idea. There are lots of subtle, streak-free products to choose from, and provided you've exfoliated and moisturized first you should avoid disasters. I always think it's safer to fake tan the night before an event to avoid smelling of tan solution and if you wake up to a patchy result there is still time to remedy the problem.

···› A glass of warm milk just before bed really does work. Milk contains tryptophan, which is proven to help you sleep.

···› Before you settle down, rub a moisturizing hand cream into your hands and feet and slip on a pair of cotton gloves and socks. These will help the cream work super-efficiently and you'll wake in the morning with really soft, smooth skin.

DID YOU KNOW?
Waxing isn't a good idea just before an event, when you want to look your best. Although a bikini wax will make you feel infinitely more sexy, you're usually left with a rash for at least 24 hours afterwards.

Next day

Last night was all about recovery and rest. Today it's time to invigorate. Kick-start the day with a mug of hot water and a squeeze of lemon juice.

···᠈ Next, breakfast – the most important meal of the day. You need to eat to fuel yourself for everything you're doing later, and breakfast helps to wake up your metabolism. Opt for a bowl of high-fibre cereal, wholegrain toast or porridge.

···᠈ Try *eating* your fruit juice. In place of a glass of orange juice eat an orange, kiwi fruit or strawberries. You'll cut calories, add fibre – which will help to fill you up – and still take in more than twice your recommended quota of vitamin C.

···᠈ Drink plenty of water throughout the day. If your body is properly hydrated, you'll quickly see an improvement in the appearance of your skin.

···᠈ Swap your coffee and regular tea for green tea. The antioxidants and flavonoids in it will boost your metabolism and help you burn up extra calories.

···᠈ Exercise is another good way of waking up your body. To give your skin a healthy glow at the same time, take a brisk walk through the park or by the river. Look around you and take a few long, deep breaths. Admit it, you're already feeling more alive. And all those endorphins you've released will stay with you for the next eight hours.

···᠈ Plan what you're going to wear later. Don't leave it to the last minute. I don't think it's wise to buy a new outfit at this stage. You'll rush, panic, get flustered and make mistakes. Accessories are a different matter, though, so why not choose a new belt, a piece of jewellery, a pretty scarf, even a handbag or pair of shoes to lift and update your clothes. If you do buy new shoes, make sure they are comfortable. Discomfort will affect your posture and can be ageing. If you have a choice of outfits, always try to incorporate some colour, either in the clothes or with accessories. Colour throws light against your face and will help give you that all-important youthful glow.

···᠈ And don't forget underwear, which includes decent tights or stockings. You'll know what you're wearing underneath and it will make a real difference to how attractive you feel.

···⟩ You want to avoid overfilling your stomach and snacking, but even if your old black dress is a bit of a squeeze, don't miss meals. At lunchtime eat a piece of fruit before your meal. This will help to fill you up and make you less likely to snack later. Soup is a good choice because it's satisfying but low in calories. Add a little protein as it takes longer to digest and keeps you feeling full for longer – chicken or fish would both be good choices. Remember to keep on drinking water – at least 2 litres!

···⟩ Body brush to massage your skin, get the blood flowing and stimulate your circulation, then take a warm shower. Wash and condition your hair, unless you've booked an appointment with the hairstylist. Remember to moisturize immediately afterwards, while your skin is still damp, to lock in moisture.

···⟩ Think about a facial. This could be as simple as a rejuvenating, moisturizing face mask at home, or a salon treatment. Products used professionally are usually more potent and effective than those you buy for home use, so the results will be that bit more dramatic. You must make it clear from the outset that you want a reviving facial that will leave your skin glowing and ready to party, rather than a harsher treatment – that can wait for another day.

···⟩ This is not the best time to change your hair colour or get a radical new cut, but a professional blow-dry or style, especially if you want to wear your hair up, is well worth the money. If you are thinking about doing something more dramatic yourself, like an up-style, it's always better to wash your hair the night before, as otherwise your hair will be too soft and difficult to handle.

···⟩ Don't forget your finger- and toenails if they're going to be on show. File and shape them and slick on nail polish. You could match the colours on your fingers and toes, or opt for a more subtle look with clear or pale pink for your fingers. Either way, make sure your nails aren't too long and that any nail polish is well applied. Smudges and uneven colour do not create an attractive look.

···⟩ Shape and pluck your eyebrows. Nothing lifts the face more effectively and your eyes will instantly look more open. Colour eyebrows with a soft powder, using an eyebrow brush for the best effect. You'll be surprised how easy it is to give shape and definition to your face this way.

⋯⟩ Take time over your make-up, but don't make the mistake of applying too much, even for an evening out. Rather than looking glamorous, you'll just look older. Youthful beauty is all about fresh, clear, glowing skin and bright eyes. Another tip is to emphasize either your eyes or your lips, *not both*. Eyelash curlers are essential for widening your eyes and making the most of your lashes. Concealer is also vital because it hides dark shadows, brightens your eyes and wipes out any broken veins or blemishes.

⋯⟩ Play fun music while you're dressing to get you in the mood. Remember the fun you had when you were a teenager getting ready with friends?

⋯⟩ Choose your favourite perfume and dab it onto the pulse points on your inner wrists, behind your ears and in the hollow at the base of your neck. For an all-over scent, spray the air immediately in front of you and step through the mist. And before you go, take one last look in the mirror and smile at yourself. If you feel good, you will look great!

'You have to realize that before two hours of make-up, even I don't look like Cindy Crawford.'

CINDY CRAWFORD, MODEL

10-day plan

It is possible to look years younger even if you've only got 24 hours to play with. But let's face it, most of the time you're going to have a bit longer to work some magic.

Assuming you have a whole 10 days to get your act together, you can start to make a pretty significant difference to the way you look. During our first series I consistently managed to knock 10 years off our contributors in just 10 days – that's a pretty impressive year per day. If you want to achieve similarly significant results, you're going to have to commit to a plan. Ten days is plenty of time to make a difference, but not long enough to start cutting corners – if you're going to knock 10 years off in 10 days, you're going to need every single moment.

Before we get going on our 10-day plan there are a few things worth bearing in mind. I don't want you to fail, so please take these questions seriously.

Have you got ten clear days to really commit to this plan?

Honestly? Think through what you've got on over the next 10 days and be sure you haven't got something planned that will make it impossible to stick to the rules. Failing will make you feel worse than not even trying, so it would be better to wait a few weeks until the timing's right rather than rush ahead and fall at the first hurdle.

Do you have a strong enough reason for wanting to do the plan?

The people who come to me and are the most successful really *want* to lose a few years. Analyse why you want to turn back the clock. A special event? Career reasons? For your relationship? You must buy into it for yourself, not because someone else has said you should. My key message, which you should know by now, is to take control of your own life. What's your incentive? Having a real goal to aim for is a great start.

> **DID YOU KNOW?**
> Remember it takes seven days to break a habit and 10 days to make a new one.

Be realistic

If you've lived, played and worked hard for decades, you're not going to recapture your youth in just 10 days. This plan should kick-start you into a new way of living, eating and managing your life. See it as a spring clean – if you get your house looking wonderful, you're much more likely to keep it tidy. With enough determination you can look noticeably better in 10 days, which will be a great incentive to keep looking after yourself for life.

Your exercise routine for the next 10 days is quite formidable if you've been inactive for ages, but it's worth it if you want to see the effects and start to feel like the new you. You don't need to splash out on gym membership or buy an exercise bike. If you're already a regular exerciser, you may be doing at least an hour's workout a day, so keep it up. However, if you've been pretty sedentary, don't rush in and burn yourself out. Start gently and increase the intensity and length of time you exercise over a period of days. You also need to include toning and flexibility exercises in your daily routine. By the end of the 10 days your body should look considerably more toned and taut.

Looking 10 years younger is about establishing the right daily routine. The 10-day plan is all about helping you do just that. If you can keep it up for 10 days, you're more likely to keep it up for life!

It's all in the preparation

Before you embark on the 10-day plan you need to do a little preparation. Time is of the essence and you don't want to waste it by trying to book appointments, buy new foods and fit in shopping sessions at the last minute.

I want you to get your hair cut and coloured in the next 10 days, and enjoy a facial, a massage *and* a pedicure if you can run to that. You should consider going to see the dentist to have your teeth attended to. Maybe you'll decide to join a gym as well. Whether you do some or all of these things, you need to make sure they fall within the 10 days. So make a list and get ready to hit the phone now to make the appointments in advance.

Nutritional supplements are a great way to fight ageing problems, so visit your local health food shop to buy some supplies, and do the same with your food shopping. You've read Chapter 7 on nutrition so you know the kind of food you should be putting inside you. Whether you're shopping just for yourself or for you and a family, planning ahead will help you stick to your new, improved diet. If you find the cupboards bare just when you start to feel peckish, there's a danger that you'll start snacking on the wrong kinds of food, so draw up a shopping list and get those lemons in.

The daily plan

Over the next 10 days I want you to stick to this daily plan (on the following page). It forms the main framework of your life for the next 10 days.

'There is no failure, except in no longer trying.'

ELBERT HUBBARD, SOCIAL PHILOSOPHER

Day 1 (the daily plan)

Morning

···⟩ Wake up your system and drink a glass of warm water with a slice or squeeze of lemon. This will kick-start your system and flush out the toxins.

···⟩ When you're in the shower, help your lymph system to drain toxins away by gently brushing your hands over your body towards your feet. Switch the warm water to cold for an invigorating blast to get your circulation going.

···⟩ If this is when you wash your hair, give it a good, deep clean, not a quick lather and rinse. Put a conditioner on and leave it for a couple of minutes while you bodybrush. Rinse thoroughly with warm water and, when your hair feels really clean, give it a final rinse with cold water.

···⟩ Slather your body with a rich moisturizer. Focus on the chest and neck areas as they can really show signs of ageing.

···⟩ Cleanse, tone and moisturize your face. Don't forget the sunscreen unless it's already incorporated into your moisturizer.

···⟩ Apply a rich eye cream in small doses.

···⟩ Eat breakfast: plenty of fibre, fruit and dairy.

···⟩ Take your daily vitamin supplements.

···⟩ Brush your teeth at least twice a day, and preferably after every meal. Use a whitening toothpaste to give yourself a sparkling smile.

···⟩ Aim to drink 2 litres of water every day. Try to drink throughout the day, rather than glug it all down last thing at night, as otherwise your sleep will be disturbed by lots of trips to the loo.

···⟩ Introduce a couple of cups of green tea to your daily routine to boost your metabolism.

···⟩ You will be eating three balanced meals a day – breakfast, lunch and dinner. Choose colourful foods such as green broccoli, red peppers, oranges, kidney beans . . . you get the picture. Eat me a rainbow (see page 190).

···⟩ Try to cut out sugar during the 10 days, and cut down your salt intake.

···⟩ Are you a smoker? If you can't give up instantly, reduce your smoking by 10 per cent on the first day. For example, if you smoke 40 a day, cut back by four on day one. Try to reduce the number you smoke a little each day, and over the next 10 days you'll see the difference in your skin.

···⟩ Exercise for at least half an hour a day. You can choose the activity – swimming, walking, running, cycling, skipping – and try to include some toning and flexibility exercises as well.

···⟩ Remember that aerobic exercise can simply be part of your normal routine. Don't take the lift, walk quickly up the stairs (and down again). Try to walk to the shops rather than drive, or at least park some distance from your destination.

···⟩ Do something enjoyable and pleasant at least once a day. Relaxing, switching off and making time for yourself are just as important as a good diet and exercise.

Evening

···⟩ Drink half a litre of cold water before bed; it increases your metabolic rate by about 30 per cent.

···⟩ Cleanse, tone and moisturize your face, then apply a rich eye cream before bed.

···⟩ Gently file around the edges of your nails.

···⟩ Put a rich moisturizing cream on your feet and hands just before bed, then slip on some cotton socks and gloves to lock the cream in.

···⟩ Cut right back on alcohol – completely if possible. If you can't go cold turkey, one glass of red wine a day is OK.

···⟩ Get an early night.

Day 2

- Cut your tea and coffee intake to one cup a day.

- Take a brisk half-hour walk, jog or cycle.

- Follow this with 20 tricep dips, 20 push-ups and 20 shoulder-sculpting exercises (see pages 122–3).

- Make sure you include some omega-3 and omega-6 foods in your diet today (see page 175).

- Have some sunflower and sesame seeds to hand in case you feel peckish between meals. No crisps or biscuits.

- Go through your make-up drawer and throw out anything that's over six months old.

- Fashion detox. Take a good look at your wardrobe and bag up all those clothes that make you feel bad, that you haven't worn for over a year, that won't ever fit you again or that date and age you. This goes for underwear and accessories as well.

- Treat yourself to some magazines. Have a look at the fashion and beauty pages to see what colours and shapes are in fashion, and pick out any looks you like and think would suit you.

- Draw up a list of five things you really like about yourself and five things you would like to change.

'As long as a woman can look 10 years younger than her daughter, she is perfectly satisfied.'
OSCAR WILDE

Day 3

···⟩ Cut out tea and coffee altogether until the
end of the plan.

···⟩ Eat some grapefruit today. Volunteers in
a US study who ate half a grapefruit or drank
a glass of grapefruit juice three times a day
found they lost an average of 1.5 kg in three
months without having to eat any less.
Beware, though, as grapefruit juice can react
with some medication; check with your GP.

···⟩ Try for around 40 minutes of aerobic exercise
today. Have you tried swimming? It's a great
exercise for the whole body, especially if you
have problems with your joints or bones.

···⟩ Drop all your wardrobe rejects off at the
nearest charity shop. Have a good long think
about where the gaps in your wardrobe are.
Think about what colours suit you and why
a certain item makes you look so good. What
caught your eye in the magazines? You'll be
going shopping later in the week and you'll
want to know what to pick off the shelves
and what to put back.

···⟩ Take a long, hard look at yourself in the mirror
in your underwear. This is an exercise in
honesty, not in how pessimistic you can be
about yourself. What are your good points?
And which are the ones you need to conceal?
Think of it as homework before shopping.

···⟩ Toning exercise – work on your bottom
today. At least 10 leg lifts and 10 squats
(see page 130).

···⟩ Treat yourself to a big bunch of flowers
to brighten up your home.

···⟩ Exfoliate your face. You only need to do this
once a week; any more than this and you're
being too tough on your delicate facial skin.
One of the best exfoliators is a flannel and
face wash (not soap). Be gentle and don't
stretch the skin – you're only trying to get
rid of the dead skin cells to reveal the fresh
skin beneath. Follow with a moisturizing
face mask.

···⟩ If you're feeling a bit achy after all this
exercising and toning, add some Epsom
salts to your evening bath and have a
relaxing soak. Make sure to moisturize
well afterwards.

···⟩ Have a relaxing herbal tea before bed.

Day 4

⤍ At breakfast, sprinkle some seeds and nuts on your porridge or cereal. They're packed full of essential fatty acids and antioxidants and will give you energy and vitality that will show up in your complexion.

⤍ Back exercises today – 10 on each leg (see page 127).

⤍ You should have increased your aerobic exercise by another five minutes; that's at least three quarters of an hour. Don't have time for the full 45? Try a 20-minute walk before work or at lunchtime, then cycle or swim later in the day. Just make sure to raise that heartbeat and get your blood pumping.

⤍ If you can do a full 45-minute session, try some interval training. That means working out hard for a couple of minutes, then easing off a little and repeating the pattern throughout the session. This burns more calories than working at the same rate all the time.

⤍ Have a facial today. This can be a DIY session or a salon treatment. Having one today will ensure you get over any outbreaks by day 10.

⤍ Get a professional to shape your eyebrows or, if you feel confident, do it yourself. This opens up your eyes and gives you an instant brow lift. Again, doing this today will make sure that any redness will have subsided by the final day.

⤍ One more day till your shopping trip. Is this 10-day programme leading up to a special occasion? Do you know what you're going to wear? If you're not planning anything special, treat yourself to a great everyday outfit.

⤍ Make a list of all the things you need and set yourself a budget. This will help you stay focused. Set aside any clothes you need to find things to go with. Don't forget to wear a good bra and comfortable shoes, and if you're shopping for something you'd normally wear heels with, take them along as well.

⤍ Prepare your feet for their pedicure in a few days' time. Give yourself a foot scrub to get rid of dead, hard skin, then moisturize.

⤍ Go to the cinema with friends, or rent a video, curl up and enjoy.

Day 5

Halfway there already. Well done. As a treat, you get to hit the shops today.

Try an energizing, revitalizing fruit smoothie for breakfast today.

Give yourself a full bodybrush massage in the shower this morning to get rid of toxins, and boost your circulation and lymphatic system. Moisturize afterwards.

Before you leave the house, change the bedding so you've got fresh, clean, crisp sheets to relax into when you get home after a long day at the shops.

Go for a swim – 50 minutes if you can manage it; if not, 30 minutes, then add 20 minutes of brisk walking later in the day – followed by a sauna before you go shopping. The swim will boost your energy and the sauna will help eliminate even more toxins.

Go shopping – alone. This is your time and your plan. If you're still not entirely sure what outfit or items you're after, treat this as a serious recce mission. Try things on, remember where you saw them, then go home and think about whether they follow my fashion advice and will take the years off you, rather than put them on.

If you are buying, don't buy anything that doesn't make you feel fantastic. No matter how basic an item, if it doesn't make you feel good, it won't make you feel younger.

Avoid lifts. Walk up escalators and stairs. Your bottom and thighs will thank you for it in the end.

You will probably be tired when you get home. Help yourself to relax, and for greater flexibility and toning, do 40 obliques (side stretches), 20 on each side (see page 128).

Look through all your old photo albums – they're guaranteed to raise a smile. Did we really choose those hairstyles and clothes?

Light some candles, burn some incense or essential oils, such as lavender, marjoram or mandarin, and have a long soak in the bath. Really pamper yourself and your senses.

Day 6

→ Toning exercise – 20 stomach crunches or tenses (see page 128) plus 20 tricep dips (see page 123).

→ Exercise today – you should be up to nearly an hour's worth of aerobic exercise. Today, try to do your exercising in one uninterrupted session.

→ Book yourself in for a bra fitting. Your boobs change shape and size throughout your life, so it's important to make sure they're getting the right support. A good bra can take kilos off you.

→ Give your hair a treat tonight and apply a deep-conditioning hair mask. You've got an appointment with the hairdresser in a couple of days, so don't wash it tomorrow. A good shampoo and condition tonight will be preparation enough.

→ Introduce some raw food into your diet today – carrot and celery sticks to nibble on are a good idea.

→ Try not to eat any carbs after 6 p.m. This can really help you cut the calories and get the weight off more quickly, especially if you're fairly inactive in the evenings.

→ Remember the child inside you? Rediscover it today. Have a pillow fight or blow some bubbles.

'I have everything I had 20 years ago, except now it's all lower.'

GYPSY ROSE LEE, ENTERTAINER

Day 7

⋯⇢ Time for a leg, bikini and underarm wax … if you can manage all three at once. Shave if you must, but you'll really see the difference if you start getting a professional wax, and it's the best preparation for a smooth tan, which you'll be doing on day nine.

⋯⇢ Spend time trying on your new clothes. Write down all the combinations that work for you as a quick reference guide when you're stuck for inspiration in the morning. Make a list of accessories that you may need to finish off each outfit. Remember that the right jewellery, bag, shoes or scarf can draw the eye away from problem areas and make you look more youthful.

⋯⇢ Make-up shopping today. Treat yourself to a free make-up session in one of the department stores. Go for a high-quality brand; you can always buy similar colours from a cheaper brand later. Ask for advice on which colours and textures you should wear, explaining what your own style is so that you will feel comfortable with the final look. For impartial advice, you could book a session with a make-up artist in the comfort of your own home.

⋯⇢ Even if you feel tired after all that shopping and exercising, make time for a long walk (about an hour) to work those muscles, boost your circulation and raise your heart rate. If a whole hour is going to be difficult, divide the time into manageable sessions throughout the day, such as two 30-minute or three 20-minute sessions.

⋯⇢ Is the thought of exercising getting you down? Exercise releases endorphins in your brain – chemicals that actually make you feel happier – so that exercise gets easier the more you do.

⋯⇢ For toning today, try isometric exercises (see page 130). Isometrics is a fancy name for clenching muscles to tone them and can be done almost anywhere. Try squeezing your bottom really tightly for a count of five, then release and do them again … and again. Do at least 20, or as many as you can in a minute.

⋯⇢ For your evening bath, imagine you're Elizabeth Taylor playing Cleopatra: put powdered milk in the running water; it's great for your skin.

Day 8

---> Wear one of your new outfits and make-up styles today.

---> Go to your hairdresser for a cut and colour to take years off you. Ask them what they think you should do with your hair. Explain your lifestyle to them (if you haven't got time to do more than wash and go in the morning, there's no point in adopting an elaborate style). Listen to their advice and don't be too shy to ask for a lesson in how to blow-dry your hair to watch the years fall off.

---> Waist and stomach exercises today (see pages 128–9).

---> This is a vitamin C day – make sure that you have at least one food containing vitamin C with each meal (see page 181).

---> Have a blitz on cellulite today. There are some fabulous new anti-cellulite gels and creams on the market, or you could treat yourself to a full body massage at a salon.

---> Give yourself a facial today. Make your own by mashing cucumber with natural yoghurt. Leave on for 15 minutes and then rinse off. It's a great pick-me-up for skin.

---> Your exercise today is dancing. Yes, socialize while you exercise. You won't even realize you're working out – Julia Roberts swears by it. If you don't fancy going out for a boogie, draw the curtains, turn on the music, sashay around the living room and rediscover your inner teenager.

---> A glass of red wine to help you dance the night away wouldn't go amiss either.

Day 9

⸱⸱⸱▸ Your toning exercise today is simple: take the stairs two at a time for a thorough thigh and bottom workout. If you live in a bungalow, don't cheat. Go out and find some stairs.

⸱⸱⸱▸ Don't give up on exercise just because the end is in sight. These last two days could really boost your muscle tone. You don't need to increase the amount of time you exercise aerobically, but try to turn up the intensity a notch or two.

⸱⸱⸱▸ This is the day your feet have been looking forward to. Today they get a pedicure (either at home or in a salon) or a trip to a chiropodist.

⸱⸱⸱▸ A sun-kissed look makes us all feel great and look good. A fake tan is a sure way to look healthy and relaxed without all the harmful rays from the sun. You can either apply it yourself, get a friend to help or go to a salon. If you apply it today, you'll still look freshly bronzed tomorrow and won't smell 'fake' either.

⸱⸱⸱▸ Have a light evening meal – nothing too heavy. Maybe some grilled chicken or fish with a few steamed vegetables.

⸱⸱⸱▸ Write a list of things you want to have achieved by this time next year. They can be sensible or silly, large or small. Now pick 10 of them and plan to work your way through that list.

⸱⸱⸱▸ Have an early night. You don't want to look drawn and tired tomorrow.

Day 10

--→ Start the day with a really brisk walk, jog, cycle or session at the gym for an hour.

--→ Toning today will concentrate on your pelvic floor (see page 129).

--→ A refreshing morning shower rather than a soak in the bath will ensure your tan stays in place.

--→ Make sure you have everything ready for your big occasion: jewellery, make-up, tights, nail polish, clothes, etc, then lay them all out ready to be put on.

--→ Put on your favourite, upbeat music while you get ready.

--→ Take the phone off the hook and allow at least two hours to get ready.

--→ Give yourself a manicure and paint your fingernails and toenails, if required.

--→ Give yourself a face mask and pop a couple of slices of cucumber on your eyes while you let it take effect.

--→ Apply your make-up, style your hair and finish up with a squirt of your favourite scent.

--→ Look in the mirror. Remember that face and body 10 days ago. Now look at what you've achieved.

You're fitter, leaner, healthier and more relaxed. You've worked your way through 10 pretty rigorous and demanding days. You might have tried something new for the very first time, or perhaps you've rediscovered good habits that fell by the wayside some time ago. Whatever the case, you've taken huge steps forward.

The 10 days are over, but hopefully some – if not all – of the plan will stick with you. If nothing else, the daily plan should become a way of life rather than a chore. You should be feeling and looking younger. Over the next few weeks and months, if you find you've slipped a little, return to the 10-day plan and book another session with yourself. Take another 10-day challenge and see if you can look 10 years younger.

6-week plan

Everyone has bad habits. But guess what? Bad habits are something we pick up and teach ourselves; we aren't born with them. That means bad habits can be unlearned, and you've got six weeks to start stamping out as many of them as possible.

You've got the tools, the facts and the inspiration in this book. Need help with eating habits? A reminder why drinking water is such a good idea? A quick flick through this book will tell you what you need to know.

Remind yourself constantly of the reasons why you want to change and how much better your life will be. Plan ahead as much as possible to help stay motivated. Six weeks sounds quite a long time, but it's easily achievable. Break it down into short-term goals – small steps rather than big leaps – and don't be put off by setbacks along the way; stay focused on the goal.

DID YOU KNOW?
If you drink five or more glasses of water a day you cut your risk of heart disease by 40 per cent. » Running for the bus, walking the dog and doing the weekly shop all burn 100,000 calories a year. » Research has discovered that 57 per cent of us feel highly stressed during an average week.

This is a tough plan, so at the end of each week I want you to reward yourself with something. It doesn't have to be a diamond ring the size of a duck egg – although that would be nice – it can be something small, like a nice smelly candle, a pair of shoes, a bunch of flowers. Whatever lifts your spirits. Go on, treat yourself, you deserve it.

I don't mean you should throw yourself into a mad frenzy of weights, kickboxing and triathlon eventing – that's a sure way to put you off exercise for life. Perhaps you already exercise a bit but didn't realize it. Walking the dog burns up to 200 calories an hour, a decent jog 500. Cycle everywhere and you burn 400 calories an hour. Brisk walks, using the stairs rather than the lift, doing the housework – it all helps.

If you haven't done any exercise for a while, if ever, start off gently. For example, try alternating between walking for 3 minutes and jogging for 60 seconds for a total of 18 minutes. As you get fitter, decrease your walking time in favour of running. If you're worried about whether your knees will hold up, avoid things like running, jogging and tennis and stick to swimming or cycling. If you already exercise, consider upping the intensity a bit, or swapping your weekly swim with another activity.

Thirty minutes, three times a week is the minimum to maintain physical health. If you can't do a full half hour, divide your exercise up into more manageable mini sessions. Three 10-minute sessions a day has a more positive effect on your body than nothing at all.

Put the exercise sessions in your diary and stick to them like appointments. Keep a record of how far you walked, ran or swam. Compare the results at the end of six weeks. As well as an improved score, you should feel fitter and see the difference. Three or four fitness sessions a week would be brilliant, but don't do them all in one go. Keep a day of rest between each session. If you don't rest, you can do more harm than good and over-exercising can actually age you.

I'm not going to ask you to jump in at the deep end right from day one. Let's break ourselves into this sensibly and relatively gently. I don't want you to think that you are going on a diet; it's more a case of changing your diet to suit your new lifestyle. Before you start, review your weekly shop – you're aiming to buy fewer ready meals and processed foods than you would normally.

Try to choose fresh produce that's as near to its original form as possible. If you can, buy organic food. Brightly coloured fruit and veg contain antioxidants, which slow the ageing process by keeping wrinkles at bay, boost collagen production and keep your cells, tissues and blood vessels healthy. Red,

purple, orange and dark green fruits and vegetables are the best anti-ageing foods.

Reduce the size of the portions you normally eat and you'll find that you lose weight. It's also important to have a cut-off point for eating in the evening. You'd be surprised by how many hundreds of calories a day a night-time nibble can add on.

Research has discovered that 57 per cent of us feel highly stressed during an average week, but most of us find unhealthy ways of dealing with it, such as reaching for a cigarette, a drink or a packet of biscuits. Rising to a challenge is one thing, continued stress and tension is quite another. We all have busy lifestyles, so we have to learn to wind down and relax. Don't get stressed by this six-week plan. It's not a test to win or fail at; it's a way of life to help you feel good about yourself, so enjoy your achievements as the days go by.

Once a week, have a good, long, hard look in the mirror. This is *not* so you can beat yourself up about what you see. Remember the power of positive, optimistic thought? Focus on what you would like to change and then see how it changes and improves as the weeks go by. Use that positive change to encourage you to keep going.

Get ready

This six-week plan is all about leaving behind your bad habits and acquiring good ones. The aim is to create a healthy lifestyle and an approach to living that supports you when the going gets tough or you simply aren't in the mood to stick to a plan.

You know what's coming. I've talked about these strategies throughout the book: exercise more, eat healthily, relax, enjoy yourself and you can make yourself look 10 years younger. The following plan is a guide to help you build up that supportive system. Some of the points should be carried through the whole six weeks – such as giving up smoking – while other points can be changed for another exercise when one week finishes. You'll get the idea as you read through.

Week 1

···⟩ Cleanse and moisturize your skin both morning and night. By the end of the six weeks this should have become a habit. You'll also be giving your skin some extra treats throughout the six weeks to give you a real glow.

···⟩ Get off the bus a stop earlier or park the car a walk from the office or shops. Getting active in the morning wakes up the body and gets your heart rate going so that you're ready to face the day, and if you get your exercise session out of the way you won't have to worry about it for the rest of the day. Use your exercise sessions this week to problem solve – put on some headphones and listen to your favourite music. Not only does it help pass the time, but studies show that it helps to organize your thoughts and may even make you brainier.

···⟩ Think young. Ageing is a state of mind. Thrills make life fun and will keep you young, but don't leave off the seatbelt, drive over the speed limit or avoid medical check-ups.

···⟩ Cut your tea and coffee intake down to one or two cups a day. Drink at least 1.5–2 litres of water a day. Cut down on salt as it dehydrates the body by drawing water out of the cells and drying tissues, including your skin. Excessive salt intake has even been associated with stomach cancer and high blood pressure.

···⟩ Plan your meals this week so you don't find yourself absolutely starving with nothing healthy to nibble. If that happens, you'll find yourself reaching for all sorts of unsuitable things. Ideally, you want three main meals a day, with two snacks (one in the morning and one in the afternoon). 'Snacks' doesn't mean a packet of crisps, by the way. Try a handful of dried apricots, an apple, chopped up peppers or some nuts to keep hunger at bay.

···⟩ Cut out smoking. For every minute you smoke, a minute of your life is taken away. Smoking ages the heart, skin and lungs; it can trigger early menopause, heart disease, cancer and osteoporosis. Need I say more?

···⟩ Do breathing exercises after work and at the end of the day. They relax you and make you feel more energized. One exercise is called 'belly breathing'. Breathe in and imagine the breath travelling all the way through your body and inflating your abdomen. When you exhale, your tummy goes flat.

···⟩ Bodybrushing or exfoliating gives your skin a wonderful smoothness and helps drainage and cell renewal. Make sure you moisturize immediately afterwards, but don't get carried away. If you exfoliate more than twice a week, you can dehydrate your skin and make it more sensitive. Incorporate this into your routine at least once a week.

--→ Put an intensive conditioner on your hair after shampooing at least once a week from now on.

--→ Put aside an evening a week to use a face mask. Incorporate this into your weekly routine from now on. Get one from the chemist or beauty counter, or you could make your own. Your skin will look glowing afterwards.

--→ Another thing to help your skin glow is regular sex. If sex has fallen somewhere between 'take the rubbish out' and 'spring clean garage', move it up your list of things to do – it deserves higher priority. Sex boosts your heart and your immune system, as well as triggering the brain to release growth hormones that have an anti-ageing effect on your body.

--→ Believe in yourself. If you don't, you won't have a chance of succeeding at this plan. You've already taken several giant, positive steps forward by just reading through this book and making changes, so let's keep going. Just be aware of what you're thinking this week – what are your thoughts about your diet and your self-image? Are they positive or negative? What have you achieved in the past that you're proud of? Use those past experiences, no matter how big or small, to help you realize that you are capable of achieving the things you want.

--→ Don't eat carbohydrates after 5 p.m., don't have caffeine or alcohol after 9.30 p.m., and try to sleep for seven or eight hours a night – quality sleep is essential for rejuvenation and repair; you'll notice the difference in a fortnight.

--→ Write down a list of words that you feel describe you in relation to the roles you play in your life, your physical characteristics, your relationships and your abilities. Pick 10 of the most important descriptions of who you are and put them in order of importance. Are they good or bad? Positive or negative? Don't be hard on yourself. The fact that you've decided to start on this six-week plan means that you're prepared to make something of yourself and your life. What aspects are there that you'd like to change? I'm going to ask you to repeat this exercise at the end of the sixth week so we can see if there are any changes.

--→ If you are a woman, at some point during these six weeks you may have a period. For many of us, we crave something sweet at this time. Don't feel guilty about it, have a treat. Make yourself a cup of hot chocolate – not the instant stuff: get 50 g of good-quality dark chocolate and heat it in a pan with 330 ml milk. Stir constantly. Plain chocolate contains magnesium, antioxidants and healthy compounds that help boost energy levels and your mood, and are good for your heart.

Week 2

⋯⋙ Get a pedometer and measure how many steps a day you do – 10,000 a day really helps weight loss and keeps you fit. Add some toning exercises for your legs to streamline your thighs, calves and ankles. Increase your exercise workout by another five minutes.

⋯⋙ Continue to eat three meals a day with a mid-morning and afternoon snack. This will keep your blood-sugar levels balanced, which will help you lose weight and reduce cravings. Fatty foods contain galanin which, when we eat it, increases our desire for fat, so we get into a vicious cycle. That's why, sadly, fatty foods are nice to eat. If you're worried about cravings, don't snack on doughnuts; have some 'good' fats to hand, as in nuts and seeds.

⋯⋙ Reduce caffeine intake to two cups of tea and coffee a day. Cut back on alcohol – start by limiting yourself to one glass of beer or wine (preferably red) a day. Go for quality, not quantity. If it's easier, cut out booze entirely for six weeks. Check out your wee; it should be getting paler and more plentiful now because you're keeping yourself well hydrated. If it's dark and looks like apple juice, you're not getting enough fluid (some medications can affect the colour of urine, so bear this in mind).

⋯⋙ Switch from white to brown. Wholegrains are rich in thiamine (vitamin B), without which we get moody and irritable, which is very ageing.

The more brown, complex carbohydrates we consume, the less likely we are to crave sugar. Refined foods such as white bread, rice, cakes and biscuits; coffee, tea and alcohol encourage the elimination of water through the kidneys, which adds to the toxic overload that can show up in your skin, causing lines and wrinkles.

⋯⋙ Give yourself a relaxing hand massage. Massage the skin between your thumb and forefinger. Acupuncturists say that this draws chi energy down from the head into the rest of your body, helping to relieve headaches.

⋯⋙ Use eye cream twice a day to zap wrinkles and soften lines. You'll see a difference by the end of the six weeks.

⋯⋙ Invest in a good body cream. Look for products that contain: retinol (vitamin A, which maintains skin's health); coenzyme Q10 (found naturally in skin, it prevents damage to collagen caused by free radicals); copper (found naturally in the skin, it improves firmness but reduces with age); lactobionic acid (draws moisture from the atmosphere to keep skin hydrated and fights free radicals).

⋯⋙ Notice how you describe yourself to other people; it can be very revealing and show what you actually think of yourself. Your aim is to project an image of someone who is successful and believes in herself.

Week 3

Halfway there now. Keep an eye on the prize – a new, more youthful-looking you. Motivate yourself by picturing the new, slimmer, healthier you. Your clothes will fit, you'll have more energy, you'll look great, and people will want to be around you. How would you feel if you didn't reach that goal? Are you happy with your appearance right now? Do you still want to look that way in 10 years' time? Keep these thoughts in your mind as an incentive to help you succeed.

⋯⟩ Wash the car by hand, rather than using the car wash, or give the windows at home a good clean. It's cheaper and you give yourself a good upper-body workout. Add five minutes more to your exercise workout this week.

⋯⟩ Cut out caffeine and alcohol completely and replace with dandelion tea, a natural diuretic, which will flush toxins from your system. I'm not suggesting you never have a drink again, just be virtuous for a whole week by giving something up entirely for seven days. You will feel very proud of yourself and enjoy a glass of wine or cup of coffee all the more next week.

⋯⟩ Switch from dairy milk to calcium-enriched soya or rice milk. Have at least one 'simple' meal a day this week; for example, grilled or baked fish or lean chicken with steamed rice and one or two servings of steamed veg, such as broccoli, beans or cabbage.

⋯⟩ Invest in aromatherapy incense, candles or essential oils – ylang ylang balances fraught emotions and lavender is calming.

⋯⟩ Surround yourself with friends. Go out for an Indian or Mexican meal. Don't go wild, but spicy foods raise your body's metabolic rate and burn 50 per cent more calories.

⋯⟩ Join a yoga, t'ai chi or Pilates class. These focus on breathing in harmony with your movements – great for your energy and your complexion.

⋯⟩ Change your make-up. Visit a department store and ask an assistant to show you how to apply new colours to suit you. Clear out old cosmetics and skincare products, and invest in a new toothbrush and dental floss.

⋯⟩ Give yourself a heavy-duty hand treatment. You can indulge yourself at a beauty salon or do a home treatment. Exfoliate the skin on your hands, then massage some cream or oil into them using small, circular movements, making sure you massage each finger as well.

⋯⟩ Make an effort to stop using negative language. If you find yourself starting a sentence with a negative phrase, stop, then start again with something more positive.

⋯⟩ Have a treat. Buy the biggest bunch of flowers you can afford to brighten up your home.

Week 4

···⟫ Add five minutes more to your exercise workout this week.

···⟫ As well as your three servings of vegetables a day, add a serving of raw vegetables – you could have a carrot or celery stick as your snack, or introduce a lettuce or tomato salad to a meal.

···⟫ Invest in a great haircut. Long hair is a familiar sign of youth, but be careful with this style as you get older. Some people can carry it off, but others can't. After a certain age, long hair pulls your face down and ages you. If you don't feel you can go for the gamine look, keep some length but chop it off at the jaw line. If you're reluctant to go for a radical change, ask an expert. When you go to your hairdresser, ask them to show you two or three different ways to wear your hair.

···⟫ Start to develop visualization techniques to wind down after work or when things get a bit hectic. Close your eyes. Take deep, measured breaths. Imagine yourself in a beautiful place (a beach, a wood, by the river). Focus on the colours you can see, the sounds around you and the smells you might expect. How does your body feel in this place? Concentrate on the images and try to stay there for five minutes. This can help you get to sleep too, and deep sleep is when cell repair takes place, helping your skin keep a youthful glow.

···⟫ Target those flabby bits on your arms with specific exercises using hand weights or bottles of water (see page 123). There's nothing more ageing than wobbly flesh on upper arms.

···⟫ Have a pedicure. When your feet feel good, you feel good.

···⟫ Change your fragrance. It can be as invigorating as a new hairstyle and make you feel like a brand-new person.

···⟫ What are the well-worn negative phrases you use all the time? Write them down and start to replace them with some more positive ones.

···⟫ Surround yourself with like-minded people who share your goals and will help you stay focused. You've come this far, so don't let someone else's negative comments about what you're doing affect your confidence. Remember, you must accept responsibility for yourself. At the end of the day, how you look, what you eat and how you feel is down to you and you alone. You have the power to succeed.

···⟫ Have a treat. Cashmere is one of life's ultimate luxuries. We can't all afford a sweater, but how about a pair of socks to slip into at bedtime?

Week 5

··⇢ Continue to add five more minutes to your exercise workout this week. You may find that you have either stopped losing weight or are putting it back on. That's because you're swapping fat for toned muscle, which weighs more than flab. Your shape will be improving and, even better, for every kilo of lean muscle mass you put on, you can expect to burn up to an extra 100 calories a day.

··⇢ Aim for one wheat-free meal a day this week. For example, breakfast could be fruit with yoghurt and honey; lunch a tuna salad; and dinner chicken served with brown rice and steamed vegetables.

··⇢ Be bold and try something new. Supermarkets are full of exotic fruit and vegetables that you've probably never heard of. Pick one, find out about it and what you can do with it, then eat it.

··⇢ Nearly there. Are you up for a detox day? Jerry Hall has one a week where she just drinks water with lemon.

··⇢ Have a massage as a treat and to get rid of tension – it improves your skin, your memory and your mood. There are loads to choose from at health spas and beauty salons. If money's a bit tight, contact your local college and see if they have a beauty department: they might need models to practise on.

··⇢ Develop a positive saying or phrase that means something to you and motivates you. Mine is, 'If you believe it, you can achieve it'.

··⇢ Go for a walk in the park or by the river and breathe in the fresh air. Take some time to be by yourself and enjoy your own company.

'I never, ever look ahead. I just stagger into the future.'

KATE ADIE, TELEVISION JOURNALIST

Week 6

By adding five minutes extra to your exercise workouts each week, you've added over an hour's extra exercise to your weekly routine – how about that for an achievement?

Try green tea instead of your usual brew. Green tea speeds up metabolism, and research has shown that drinking five cups a day burns 4 per cent more calories – which could equal a weight loss of 3.5 kg a year.

Why not try a personal shopper? It sounds very Hollywood, but it's easily available to us all. Many high-street chain stores offer personal shopping services free to their customers, or treat yourself to your own personal stylist. It's a brilliant way to experiment with new looks and get a second opinion from someone other than a friend or member of your family. By now you should be noticing a difference in the way you look and feel, so celebrate by planning a new wardrobe.

Reward yourself with a facial at a beauty salon. This helps keep skin looking young because it stimulates the circulation, reduces muscle tension and makes you look rested, relaxed and youthful.

Sign up for an evening class, volunteer for a charity, join a club. Treat yourself with something fun and rewarding.

Repeat the exercise you did in the first week, where you wrote down a list of words that you felt described you in relation to the roles you play in your life, your physical characteristics, relationships and abilities. Pick 10 of the most important descriptions of who you are and put them in order of importance. Have they changed? Are they more positive? You should have at least five aspects of yourself that you are happy with, which is brilliant. Being able to take pleasure in yourself is a great achievement.

Take each week a day at a time. If it all becomes too much, aim for three achievable goals every week. For example, exercise three times, eat five portions of fruit and vegetables every day, drink more water. Then build in a bit more as and when you feel comfortable.

There will probably be times during the six weeks when it's difficult, or impossible, to follow the plan. Don't lose heart, just pick up where you left off, and if you feel you've lost a day to the plan, just add it on at the end.

Don't put your life on hold during the six weeks. Start doing what you've dreamt of doing *now*, don't wait until you're slimmer/fitter/younger-looking. If you worry about the 'what ifs' and 'buts' you'll struggle to succeed on this plan. Our self-esteem and how we feel about ourselves is entirely down to how good our self-belief is. If you *believe* you can achieve a younger-looking you, you will.

the life plan

This book is full of ideas and strategies on how to look and feel 10 years younger. Now that you've read them all and are brimming with enthusiasm, you rummage through your kitchen cupboards and throw out all the 'bad' foods and raid the health-food shops for 'good' foods, supplements and vitamins. You give your make-up bag a spring-clean. You go through your wardrobe like a dose of salts, bag up everything that isn't flattering and take it along to the charity shop. You have a go at the 24-hour plan and it's pretty easy. Ten-day plan? No sweat. What about the six-week plan? Well, a bit more of an effort but you're seeing results. And then something happens.

Gradually the enthusiasm starts to trickle away, and before you know it you're back where you started. The book is under a pile of magazines, or in the cupboard with the foot spa you never use. What happened to the life plan?

Power of mind is everything. Remember, if you believe it, you can achieve it. Think of all the people who join a gym at the beginning of the year as one of their New Year resolutions, go faithfully for a month and then stop. Why? Usually they miss a week for some reason or another, and because of this decide it isn't worth picking up where they left off. I get very frustrated with people's attitudes. If I indulge in a sticky pastry once in a while, I don't then think, 'Oh to hell with it, I'll eat anything and everything now that something naughty has passed my lips.' If you fall out of a routine, so what? Just start again, the next hour, the next day, the next week. Don't use one little lapse as an excuse to chuck it in. Get the control back and make your own decisions. You're the one in control here.

We're talking about a life plan now. Not just a short, sharp blast, forget about it and move on to the next fad/hobby/diet. If you bought this book, maybe you did so because you were stuck in a rut and it was time to change. Or maybe somebody gave you the book. What were they trying to tell you? Whatever the reason, *you* want to look 10 years younger. That's great, but it shouldn't be a chore – something to dread like going to the dentist. A life plan should be enjoyable, invigorating and uplifting, not a war on the parts of your life you hate. If it becomes a battle, the enjoyment and pleasure go out of life and it's easy to give up the struggle.

We all know that we should eat more sensibly, exercise more and learn to relax. I'm not the only one giving you that message; it's everywhere. It's good for our health and well-being and it makes us look younger. But it can be hard to stick to all the rules all at once. So don't try and do it *all at once*. Making small adjustments to your life every day can make a huge difference, and before you know it, they've become part of your life plan.

⋯⋗ Ask yourself why you want to change your life? What are the areas in your life that aren't fulfilling? Where do you think you're getting it right? Try keeping a diary of what you eat, what you feel about work/relationships and how stressed you're getting. Then you can go through it and start to improve your routine, using this book to help you. Think of your diary as a personal life plan. Jot down your weight on a certain day so you can look back and realize how much you've lost just through healthy eating, or record how many units of alcohol you normally consume – you'll feel so pleased with yourself when you realize how much you've cut back.

⋯⋗ If necessary, make appointments with yourself. Good intentions are all very well, but if you have the kind of lifestyle and personality that mean nothing gets done, write everything down in your diary or calendar. Make time for yourself.

⋯⟩ According to the Dalai Lama, the purpose of our lives is to be happy. So what makes you happy? Mood influences the body's chemical balance. Stress releases cortisol, which reduces cell renewal. Skin looks dull and wrinkled. Worry lines and frowning make us look older. The older we look, the more depressed we feel. On the other hand, if you feel good, you look good. When you feel younger, you look younger. It's really as simple as that. And now you have the tools to make yourself *look* and *feel* younger.

⋯⟩ Esther Rantzen, in her 60s, has talked about not knowing how old she is. What she means is that there are stereotypes for every age and that she feels she doesn't fit into any of them. She still loves wearing stilettos, and has even been converted to wearing thongs by her daughters.

⋯⟩ Whatever your age is now, embrace it and feel good about yourself. Don't worry about what has happened or what might happen. Think like Frank Sinatra: 'Regrets, I've had a few, but then again, too few to mention.' Don't remain locked in the past. Don't sit there thinking, 'I wish I'd done that.' Do it now. You're a human being, not a human 'doing'. Take control, change the parts of your life that you don't like, or that aren't working, or that make you unhappy.

⋯⟩ Your mind and body are yours to do whatever you want with. Don't put limits on yourself. Change shouldn't be scary. It's invigorating and a great boost to your energy levels.

⋯⟩ Put yourself first and take time for yourself. This isn't something you should feel bad about. Life won't stop just because you've decided to do something for *you*. In fact, it will have a ripple effect and benefit those around you because you'll feel less stressed, more energized and better about yourself.

⋯⟩ Getting a life plan means working out a pattern of behaviour that you can carry with you for the next 10, 20, 30, 40 years or more. Let the negative things go and embrace the positive and energizing. Live by your rules, not anyone else's. Become more dynamic and use that vitality throughout your whole life.

However, I know as well as anyone that it can be tough to battle against old habits and start a new life when everything around you has stayed the same. Your old ways seem to be screaming at you from every cupboard, sofa and wardrobe, begging you to slip back into your ageing ways. You know it's wrong for you, and that you are now feeling and looking better than you have done for years. So I want to remind you just how simple your new life is, and how much easier it is than your old one.

First, let's go through a list of all the habits you've thrown out and remind yourself that you're not going back to them. Stick them to your wardrobe, your fridge and next to your mirror, and as you read them you'll realize how much better you feel in your new life and be remotivated against the temptation of old habits. Take a look and wonder just why you did these things in the first place!

'You can take no credit for being beautiful at 16. But if you are beautiful when you are 60, it will be your own soul's doing.'

MARIE STOPES, BIRTH-CONTROL CAMPAIGNER

You will never again:

⋯⟩ Worry about getting older.

⋯⟩ Smoke – unless you want to look 10 years older and do immeasurable harm to your body.

⋯⟩ Skimp on sleep.

⋯⟩ Get stuck in a fashion rut – regularly overhaul your wardrobe, hairstyle and colour and make-up.

⋯⟩ Stay out in the sun without protection – up to 80 per cent of all signs of ageing are due to exposure to sunlight.

⋯⟩ Skip breakfast – it's the most important meal of the day and without it you can weaken your stomach and impair your digestive system – or any meal for that matter.

⋯⟩ Follow faddy diets.

⋯⟩ Think of good-quality cosmetics as out of your league – they're an investment in the future of your skin.

⋯⟩ Dress head-to-toe in one trend. Instead, mix one or two key items with plain separates.

⋯⟩ Allow sex to slip to the bottom of the list.

⋯⟩ Sleep in your make-up.

⋯⟩ Let stress take over. Find a little time each day to relax, give yourself a treat and have fun.

⋯⟩ Use negative words or thoughts. Don't put yourself or others down. You want to accentuate the positive.

⋯⟩ Think of yourself purely in physical terms – you are *so* much more than the shape and weight of your body.

⋯⟩ Say 'never'.

The truth is that we all slip. But not having time for breakfast because you had to rush the kids to school or get to a meeting doesn't mean you should throw your hands up in despair and go back to your old life. Life is difficult, and none of us are able to do everything perfectly. Just because you can't make time to exercise for a couple of days, you shouldn't punish yourself by giving up on your new ways. Just start the next day with renewed vigour. Think about all the positive steps you've made and go *with* them, not against them.

And because I don't want you to be following a set of rules, here is a list of those things you might associate with guilt and naughtiness, but which are, in fact, simply a part of normal life that should be enjoyed and relished.

You must sometimes:

⋯⟩ Drink alcohol in moderation. Enjoy a guilt-free glass of red wine – it's good for your heart, and contains all-important antioxidants to help your body fight ageing and damaging free radicals. It even contains a compound called resveratrol, which stimulates lean cells and helps shed fat.

⋯⟩ Act like the child you once were. Being young at heart keeps you looking young.

⋯⟩ Treat yourself. There's nothing wrong with chocolate, just don't wolf down the whole bar. Everything in moderation.

- Ask for help. It doesn't mean that you're any less of a human being or that you've lost control. You are there for your friends and family, so be a taker, not just a giver, from time to time.
- Take a risk.

It's easy to:
- Cleanse, tone, moisturize and protect your skin (and that includes hands and neck as well as face) daily. Choose products that suit your age and lifestyle.
- Drink plenty of water to keep your body hydrated and healthy-looking – at least eight glasses a day.
- Enjoy fresh air and oxygen. A brisk walk or bike ride in the country will do wonders for you. Research has shown that a 10-minute daily walk can help extend your life and can count as exercise.
- Exercise – a toned supple body is always going to look younger, and every system in your body is affected by exercise, or the lack of it.
- Hold yourself proudly, not like a sack of potatoes. Head up, shoulders back, walk tall.
- Brush your teeth twice a day with fluoride toothpaste, and don't forget to floss.
- Eat fruit and vegetables – especially ORAC-rich varieties (see page 203). At least five portions a day will boost your intake of antioxidants.

- Eat more fibre and choose foods from all the colour groups so that you get a full range of anti-ageing nutrients.
- Chill out – too much stress is a bad thing, so make sure you take time to unwind and relax every day.
- Write down five things that you love doing and make time to do at least one of them every month.
- Laugh – forget laughter lines and worrying about wrinkles. Laughing tones the muscles and boosts circulation to give you a healthy, natural glow.

You see, it isn't difficult, it isn't a struggle; it's about feeling happy, revitalized and above all young. Enjoy the fact that you're getting older, but don't let it run your life in a negative way. If you feel 16, why should you have to look 60? All you need is belief in the fact that you should look and feel as youthful as you want to and you'll have the capacity to do so.

Need some motivation? Take a look at how quickly small changes can have big effects, and what those old bad habits can do to you.

BAD HABITS

Smoking

⸱⸱⸱⸱⋗ Smokers' skin ages 40 per cent faster than that of non-smokers.

⸱⸱⸱⸱⋗ After only two weeks of giving up smoking your skin will improve as your circulation gets back to a normal level.

⸱⸱⸱⸱⋗ Smoking cuts your life expectancy by about 10 years – give up smoking and you can quite literally turn back the clock.

⸱⸱⸱⸱⋗ Giving up by 30 will all but reverse the damage you've done so far and give you 10 years back.

⸱⸱⸱⸱⋗ Stopping at 40 will give you nine years back and mean you'll only have reduced your life expectancy by a year.

⸱⸱⸱⸱⋗ Stopping at 50 will give you six years back.

Lack of exercise

On average, a 70-year-old's muscle strength will have reduced by a third. However, this is unnecessary and regular exercise will prevent muscle wastage and keep you toned.

Lack of sleep

⸱⸱⸱⸱⋗ Just one week of sleep deprivation (with about only four hours every night) will reduce your body's production of the hormone that controls your muscle to fat ratio, making your body more likely to store fat.

⸱⸱⸱⸱⋗ Sleep deprivation affects your digestion, so your body takes 40 per cent longer to regulate your blood-sugar levels after a high-carb meal, leaving you with high, ageing sugar levels .

Sun exposure

⸱⸱⸱⸱⋗ Up to 80 per cent of all ageing may be caused by exposure to the sun.

⸱⸱⸱⸱⋗ 90 per cent of damage caused to skin by the sun is a result of day-to-day exposure.

⸱⸱⸱⸱⋗ As soon as sunlight reaches your bare skin, it triggers the body to produce free radicals, which break down the skin's collagen, making it less elastic and prone to wrinkles or sagging.

Dehydration

Your body loses about 1.5 litres of water a day through urine, skin, lungs etc., so if you drink less than this you will literally be drying out.

Sugar

⸱⸱⸱⸱⋗ White sugar has had 90 per cent of its vitamins and minerals removed. Eat fruit for natural sugars that won't pile on the pounds.

⸱⸱⸱⸱⋗ Our diets are so full of over-processed sugar that an estimated three in ten people have uneven blood-sugar levels. Is this you?

NEW HABITS

Laughter

--> Laughter is therapy for your outsides and insides. It will tone up your facial muscles and, like a massage, increase blood flow to the areas that make your skin glow and help to fight the signs of ageing.

--> Ten minutes of laughter can significantly reduce your blood pressure, and may even help prevent heart disease by improving the circulation to your heart.

--> Studies show that one minute of intense, authentic laughter has the same stress-relieving effect as 45 minutes' deep relaxation.

--> And if you can keep laughing for a full hour you could use up an astonishing 500 calories.

Water

Increasing your water intake to 2 litres a day will have visible effects on your skin in just 24 hours. Even within this time, your skin will be smoother, softer and plumper as it's rehydrated.

Sleep

Skin cell renewal is at its maximum when you're asleep. Try to sleep on your back, which will increase the circulation of blood to your face and help fight wrinkles and eye bags.

Exercise

--> It only takes about three hours of exercise a week to see significant physical results in six to eight weeks.

--> Regular aerobic exercise can actually add seven years to your life expectancy.

--> Exercise increases the amount of oxygen your body takes up. In one study of heart-failure patients, 91-year-olds who did six months of treadmill and cycling exercise were able to massively improve their oxygen intake, and thus improve their circulation and overall health. If exercise can do this for a 91-year-old, imagine the age-defying wonders it could do for you.

--> Exercise can help depression. After exercising for only one week, mild to moderately depressed people began to feel happier, and long-term exercise continued to improve the way they felt.

--> You'll feel the happiness boost after only 20 minutes of exercise, when your body starts producing mood-boosting endorphins.

Good beauty routine

It takes 22 muscles for you to blink, wink and scrunch up your eyes when you laugh. Keep them supple and counteract the wrinkles these movements create by using a rich eye cream morning and night.

Sun protection

As 90 per cent of sun damage takes place during daily life, you can protect yourself simply by slathering on a cream containing SPF 15 or higher every day, focusing on the places that are exposed daily, such as your face, neck, chest, hands and lower arms. *Never* go without sun protection and you'll be actively combating the signs of ageing.

Good-quality nutrition

···❯ As few as five days after making improvements in your diet, you will see the difference in your skin and begin to turn back the ageing clock.

···❯ Vitamins C and E could actually help extend your life by combating ageing, even if you don't increase the levels in your diet until middle age.

···❯ Studies show that people who have a beta-carotene intake of 15–20 mg per day are 40 per cent less likely to have a stroke and 22 per cent less likely to suffer a heart attack than those with an intake of only 6 mg per day.

···❯ Green tea has the ability to lower your body's absorption of non-essential bad fats by as much as 30 per cent .

Anti-ageing lifestyle

···❯ Nearly every cell in your body is renewed over a 10-year period, and many of your bone cells are replaced every four years. By following an anti-ageing diet and lifestyle you can replace your damaged cells with fresh new ones.

···❯ Wrinkles are not inevitable: 80 per cent of them are caused by your lifestyle – the sun, pollution, smoking, drinking, late nights, bad diet – so make changes early enough and you could have only 20 per cent of the wrinkles you would have had if you'd stuck to your old habits.

···❯ We're all going to get older. I can't help you hold back time, but with this book I can help you celebrate who you are as you get older. Live life by your rules. Feel that inner glow of strength and confidence which, as it radiates outwards, gives you a youthful beauty all your own.

We talk about people growing old gracefully. What does that mean to you? For me that means a person who has embraced who they are. They live life to the full. They take care of themselves so they look and feel good. They are energetic, optimistic and positive. They don't take themselves too seriously. They're playful and fun to be around. They don't fight the fact that they are getting older. They embrace and accept the changes, and they manage to look vibrant, lively and more youthful as a result.

Most of all, don't get hung up on exactly how old you look or what others might think of you. If you're happy, you feel good in yourself and you enjoy life, you're three-quarters of the way there.

'There is a fountain of youth: it is your mind, your talents, the creativity you bring to your life and the lives of people you love. When you learn to tap into this source, you will truly have defeated age.' SOPHIA LOREN, ACTRESS

Directory

Acupuncture

British Acupuncture Council
63 Jeddo Road, London W12 9HQ
Tel: 020 8735 0400 / www.acupuncture.org.uk

British Medical Acupuncture Society (BMAS)
BMAS House, 3 Winnington Court
Winnington Street, Northwich, Cheshire CW8 1AQ
Tel: 01606 786782
www.medical-acupuncture.co.uk
To locate acupuncturists in your area

The Acupuncture Society
27 Cavendish Drive, Edgware, Middlesex HA8 7NR
Tel: 07734 668402 / www.acupuncturesociety.org.uk

Allergies

Allergy UK
3 White Oak Square, London Road, Swanley, Kent BR8 7AG
Switchboard: 01322 619898 / Allergy Helpline: 01322 619864
www.allergyfoundation.com

Alternative and Complementary Therapies

Purple Health
www.purplehealth.com
A variety of information about alternative therapies
and includes a practitioner directory

UK Therapy
www.uk-therapy.com
An online directory of therapists and practitioners in the UK.
Information on treatments, location, contact lines, fees

The Hale Clinic
7 Park Crescent, London W1B 1PF
Tel: 0870 167 6667 / www.haleclinic.com
For holistic care

Aromatherapy

International Federation of Aromatherapists
Tel: 020 8742 2605 / www.iparoma.org
For qualified aromatherapists in your area

Chiropractors

British Chiropractic Association
Tel: 0118 950 5950 / www.chiropractic-uk.co.uk
enquiries@chiropractic-uk.co.uk
The BCA represents 70 per cent of internationally accredited
UK chiropractors

Colon Hydrotherapy/Irrigation

Association and Register of Colon Hydrotherapists
www.colonic-association.org
For properly trained and insured therapists

The Guild of Colon Hydrotherapists
16 Drummond Ride, Tring, Herts HP23 5DE
Tel: 01442 823555

Cosmetic and Plastic Surgery

The British Association of Aesthetic Plastic Surgeons
The Royal College of Surgeons of England
35–43 Lincoln's Inn Fields, London WC2A 3PN
Tel: 020 7405 2234 / www.baaps.org.uk

The British Association of Cosmetic Doctors
30b Wimpole Street, London W1U 2RW
Tel: 0800 328 3613 / www.cosmeticdoctors.co.uk

The British Association of Plastic Surgeons
The Royal College of Surgeons of England
35–43 Loncoln's Inn Fields, London WC2A 3PN
Tel: 020 7831 5161 / www.baps.co.uk

Cosmetic Dentistry

British Academy of Cosmetic Dentistry
Dr Elaine Halley, Cherrybank Dental Spa
168 Glasgow Road, Perth PH2 0LY
www.bacd.com
For a directory of cosmetic dentists

British Dental Association
64 Wimpole Street, London W1G 8YS
Tel: 020 7935 0875
www.bda-dentistry.org.uk

British Dental Health Foundation
Smile House, 2 East Union Street, Rugby
Warwickshire CV22 6AJ
Helpline: 0845 063 1188 (Monday–Friday, 9am–5pm)
www.dentalhealth.org.uk

Cosmetic Dentist
Dr Surinder Hundle, Lund Osler Dental Healthcare
56 Knightsbridge, London SW1X 7JN
Tel: 020 7838 8969

Dentics
Tel: 07000 336842 / www.dentics.co.uk
Cosmetic dental studios

Tooth whitening and veneering
Tel: 0800 0768 768
For dentists who carry out this work

Exercise

Active for Life
PO Box 1489, Bristol BS99 4QJ
Tel: 0117 940 6409 / www.active-for-life.com

Fitness Industry Association
Tel: 020 7620 0700 / www.fia.org.uk
Trade organization for the entire fitness sector;
promotes excellence and best practice

The Keep Fit Association
Astra House, Suite 1.05, Arklow Road, London SE14 6EB
Tel: 020 8692 9566 / www.keepfit.org.uk

National Register of Personal Trainers
PO Box 314, Chalfont St Peter, Bucks SL9 0ZL
Tel: 0870 200 6010 / www.nrpt.co.uk

NHS Direct – Getting Active
Tel: 0845 4647 / www.nhsdirect.nhs.uk

The Ramblers' Association
Camelford House, 87–90 Embankment, London SE1 7TW
Tel: 020 7339 8500 / www.ramblers.org.uk
For details of free organized walks

Help and Advice

Action for Victims of Medical Accidents
44 High Street, Corydon, Surrey CR0 1YB
Tel: 0845 123 2352 / www.avma.org.uk

General Medical Council
London:
Regent's Place, 350 Euston Road, London NW1 3JN
Tel: 0845 357 8001
Manchester:
St James Building, 79 Oxford Street, Manchester M1 6FQ
Tel: 0845 357 8001 / Fax: 0845 357 9001
Edinburgh:
Napier House, 35 Thistle Street, Edinburgh EH2 1DY
Tel: 0131 240 6410 / Fax: 0131 220 0120
gmcscotland@gmc-org.uk

Healthcare Commission
Finsbury Tower, 103–105 Bunhill Row, London EC1Y 8TG
Tel: 020 7448 9200 / www.chai.org.uk
feedback@healthcarecommission.org.uk

iVillage
www.ivillage.co.uk
Online information network for women in the UK, focusing on
issues that matter most to women with interactive services,
expert advice, information and a support network

Medical Advisory Service
Helpline: 020 8994 9874 (Monday–Friday, 6pm–8pm)

Nursing and Midwifery Council
23 Portland Place, London W1B 1PZ
Tel: 020 7637 7181 / www.nmc-uk.org

Patient Advisory Service
Tel: 0800 068 4031 / www.patientadvisory.co.uk
Advice on cosmetic surgery

Women's Health
52 Featherstone Street, London EC1 8RT
Tel: 020 7251 6333
Helpline: 0845 125 5254 (Monday–Friday, 9.30am–1.30pm)
www.womenshealthlondon.org.uk

Women's Health Concern
PO Box 2126, Marlow, Bucks SL7 2RY
Tel: 01628 488065 / Helpline: 0845 123 2319
www.womens-health-concern.org

Holistic Facelifts

Emma Hardie Faces
Clinics in Oxford and London
Tel: 01865 516027 / www.emmahardie.com
info@emmahardie.com

Hypnotherapy

British Hypnotherapy Association
67 Upper Berkeley Street, London W1H 7QX
Tel: 020 7723 4443
www.british-hypnotherapy-association.org

Hypoxi Therapy

Hypoxi Therapy
Tel: 0800 731 1323

Isolagen

Isolagen Europe
59–61 Park Royal Road, London NW10 7JJ
Tel: 020 8453 8900 / www.isolagen.com

Medical Herbalists

British Herbal Medicine Association
1 Wickham Road, Boscombe, Bournemouth BH7 6JX
Tel: 01202 433691 / www.bhma.info

National Institute of Medical Herbalists
Elm House, 54 Mary Arches Street, Exeter EX4 3BA
Tel: 01392 426022 / www.nimh.org.uk
For qualified herbal practitioners

Meditation

Transcendental Meditation Association
Tel: 08705 143733 / www.t-m.org.uk
For information on meditation classes

Nutrition

British Association for Nutritional Therapy
27 Gloucester Street, London WC1N 3XX
Tel: 08706 061284
Send £2 plus large SAE for a list of registered
nutritional therapists

Institute for Optimum Nutrition
Blades Court, Deodar Road, London SW15 2NU
Tel: 0208 877 9993 / www.ion.ac.uk

The Nutrition Society

10 Cambridge Court, 210 Shepherd's Bush Road
London W6 7NJ
Tel: 020 7602 0228 / www.nutsoc.org.uk

Women's Nutritional Advisory Service
PO Box 268, Lewes, Sussex BN7 2QN
Tel: 01273 487366 / www.wnas.org.uk

Personal Stylist

Nicky Hambleton-Jones
Tramp2Vamp
www.tramp2vamp.com
info@tramp2vamp.com

Pilates

The Pilates Foundation UK
PO Box 36052, London SW16 1XQ
Tel: 07071 78 1859 / www.pilatesfoundation.com
For information on Pilates and qualified teachers in your area

Reflexology

Association of Reflexologists (AoR)
27 Old Gloucester Street, London WC1N 3XX
Tel: 0870 567 3320 / www.aor.org.uk
Database of members so you can find a fully qualified
reflexologist in your area

Relationships

British Association for Sexual and Relationship Therapy
Tel: 020 8543 2707 / www.basrt.org.uk
Information service and list of therapists

Relate
Herbert Gray College, Little Church Street
Rugby, Warwickshire CV21 3AP
Tel: 0845 456 1310
www.relate.org.uk

Ruthinking.co.uk
Tel: 0800 282930 / www.ruthinking.co.uk
Helpline for guidance on sex and personal relationships

Sexual Dysfunction Association
Windmill Place Business Centre
2–4 Windmill Lane, Southall, Middlesex UB2 4NJ
Helpline: 0870 774 3571 / www.sda.uk.net

Skin and Hair

**British Association of Beauty Therapy
and Cosmetology (BABTAC)**
Meteor Court, Barnett Way, Barnwood, Gloucester GL4 3GG
Tel: 0845 065 9000 / www.babtac.com

British Association of Dermatologists
4 Fitzroy Square, London W1T 6EH
Tel: 020 7383 0266 / www.bad.org.uk
For information on local NHS dermatologists

Guild of Professional Beauty Therapists
Guild House, 320 Burton Road, Derby DE23 6AF
Tel: 0870 000 4253 / www.beauty-guild.co.uk
The trade body for the UK's professional beauty salons

The Institute of Trichologists
24 Langroyd Road, London SW17 7PL
Tel: 08706 070602 / www.trichologists.org.uk

Luster haircare products
www.lusterproducts.com

National Eczema Society
Hill House, Highgate Hill, London N19 5NA
Tel: 0207 281 3553
Helpline: 0870 241 3604 (Monday–Friday, 8am–8pm)
www.eczema.org

Perricone Cosmeceuticals
Dr Nicholas Perricone
Tel: 020 7329 2000 / www.nvperriconemd.co.uk

Space NK
200 Great Portland Street, London W1W 5QG
Tel: 020 7299 4999 / www.spacenk.co.uk
Skincare, haircare, make-up and cosmetics

Universal Contour Wrap
Tel: 01784 251177
www.universalcontourwrap.co.uk

Sleep

Insomnia Helpline
Tel: 020 8994 9874 (Monday–Friday, 6pm–8pm)
For help and support

The London Snoring Centre
Tel: 020 7467 8493 / www.londonsnoringcentre.com
For advice and help for heavy snorers

Spas and Health Farms

Body Experience
Tel: 020 8334 9999 / www.bodyexperience.co.uk

British International Spa Association (BISA)
Tel: 01580 212954 / www.spaassociation.org.uk

Hoar Cross Hall
Hoar Cross, Staffs DE13 8QS
Tel: 01283 575671 / www.hoarcross.co.uk

Ragdale Hall Health Hydro
Ragdale Village,1 Melton Mowbray, Leicestershire LE14 3PB
Tel: 01664 43483 / www.ragdalehall.co.uk

Spa Break UK
Coltsford Mill, Mill Lane, Oxted, Surrey RH8 9DG
Tel: 01883 724843 / www.spabreak.co.uk
Spa resort travel agent for health spas, health farms
and spa breaks throughout the UK

Spa Seekers
Jastan House, 40 Moor Street, Coventry CV5 6EQ
Tel: 08708 50 55 50 / www.spaseekers.co.uk
Health farm and day spa advisory and central
reservation service

Stress

International Stress Management Association
PO Box 348, Waltham Cross EN8 8ZL
Tel: 07000 780430 / www.isma.org.uk

Yoga

The British Wheel of Yoga
25 Jermyn Street, Sleaford, Lincs NG34 7RU
Tel: 01529 306851 / www.bwy.org.uk
To find classes in your area

Yoga Biomedical Trust
90–92 Pentonville Road, London N1 9HS
Tel: 020 7689 3040 / www.yogatherapy.org

Index

Acknowledgements

Nicky would like to thank Alexandra Fraser and Karen Dolby, without whom this book wouldn't have materialized; Mark Read, for his magic touch and for making me look so fabulous; and Alex and Emma at Smith & Gilmour, for doing such a wonderful job designing the book.

Alexandra and Karen would like to thank the following people for their invaluable contributions: Helen Pope, for working way beyond the call of duty; the fantastic *10 Years Younger* production teams, especially Colette Foster, Serena Kennedy, Donna Mulvey, David Smith, Merrisa Merry and Chloe Nisbet; everyone at Maverick, especially the lovely Anna Mathers , Lucy Cattel and Clare Welch for making things happen and keeping things on track; also Katherine Lapworth and Meg Sanders, for all their hard work and professionalism.

Simply, the book could not have happened without the above.
Sorry if it's aged you all somewhat!

The publishers would also like to thank the following: Body Experience, for use of their health spa (tel: 020 8334 9999, www.bodyexperience.co.uk); Heidi Klein, for the swimsuits (tel: 020 7259 9426, www.heidiklein.co.uk); The Park Club, for use of their swimming pool and grounds (tel: 020 8743 4321, www.mytpc.com); Agnés B, for letting us go shopping (tel: 020 7565 1188, www.agnesb.com); and Martyn Gayle, Aveda Lifestyle Store, for wash and blow-dry (tel: 020 7243 6047, www.aveda.com).

About the author

Nicky Hambleton-Jones is a TV presenter, personal stylist and
MD of style consultancy Tramp2Vamp (www.tramp2vamp.com).
She is also a qualified dietician, and ran a nutrition practice in her
native South Africa before moving to the UK in 1996. After spending
four years working as a management consultant in the City, she
realized she was far more passionate about fashion and helping other
people to feel good about themselves. She decided to combine the
two and, in 2001, she established Tramp2Vamp. Nicky and her team
of stylists work with men and women all over the UK to help them
develop their own personal style and look fantastic effortlessly.

Tired of being thirty, feeling twenty, but looking forty? Well, fear not. Nicky Hambleton-Jones, expert presenter of the hit Channel 4 series *10 Years Younger*, is here to help.

Amazingly, the British public spend hundreds of millions of pounds a year on their appearance, so it's clear that we'd all like to know how to put the brakes on the ageing process. But with the multitude of lotions, potions and treatments available, it's hard to know exactly what to do. Is botox best? Can prunes actually provide a head start in the race against wrinkles? And does having a positive mental attitude *really* help?

Aimed at people of all ages, shapes and sizes, and packed with expert advice on everything from changing your hairstyle to eating your way to better skin, this jargon-free guide to looking and feeling your best is bursting with insider knowledge from the cream of the beauty and fashion worlds. So, whether you're looking for a twenty-four-hour quick fix or a long-term life-changing plan, this is the book for you. With the right knowledge at their fingertips, everyone can look and feel fantastic, so get reading and find out just how easy it is to look – and feel – 10 years younger.

A CHANNEL 4 BOOK

ISBN 1-905-02605-6

£12.99

Cover image © Liquid tv

9 781905 026050 >

www.booksattransworld.co.uk

MAVERICK
television